Middle Eastern Cuisine

Around the Table with The Catholic Foodie

Jeff Young

Middle Eastern Cuisine

Around the Table

with The

Catholic Foodie

Jeff Young

All photos courtesy the author except as noted.

Library of Congress Cataloging-in-Publication Data

Young, Jeff, 1970-

  Around the table with the Catholic Foodie : Middle Eastern cuisine / Jeff Young.—First edition.

208 pages cm

  ISBN 978-0-7648-2529-3 (p)— ISBN 978-0-7648-6974-7 (e)

1. Cooking, Middle Eastern. I. Title. II. Title: Middle Eastern cuisine.

 TX725.M628Y66 2014

 641.5956—dc23

2014031318

Table of Contents

Table of Contents—continued

Dedication

To my beautiful bride Charlene. You have inspired me to become so much more than I ever thought I could be. You have taught me to love, and helped me to stretch and to grow. You have taught me to taste and to appreciate good food. I have learned so much from you about cooking, about faith, and about life. Thank you for who you are, and for all the love and encouragement you give to me. You are magic, Baby! I love you!

Praise for Around the Table
with The Catholic Foodie

Jeff Young's *Catholic Foodie™* apostolate remains one of my favorite resources for nurturing and encouraging Catholic families. As a frequent listener to Jeff's show and someone who has had the opportunity to work in partnership with Jeff, I've seen firsthand the impact of his work on individuals and families. This cookbook provides yet another facet to his service on behalf of the Church and families. I can't wait to share it with our *CatholicMom.com* family and to see the impact it will have on individuals and families.

Lisa Hendey
Founder of *CatholicMom.com*,
speaker, and author

With the rise of foodies and *Food Network* stars, it's nice to see a Catholic family man who makes the connection between food, faith, family, and fun. Through this book and his web site, Jeff Young, The Catholic Foodie™, offers not only recipes and meal ideas, but inspiration to make faith and family the center of our lives. It's ironic that in today's "connected" world, our overbooked schedules and digital addictions can "disconnect" us from God and from those we love. Catholic families need The Catholic Foodie™ to remind us how important family mealtime is.

Danielle Bean
Editor-in-Chief, *Catholic Digest* magazine

The cuisine of the Holy Land is unique, with a great variety of local dishes made in our homes and adorning our tables during family gatherings, social functions, and during holidays and feasts. Food is history and culture. Food brings people together from all over the world, no matter their background, religion, the color of their skin, or their beliefs. It is beautiful to see human beings sitting together at table, talking and eating. Through food we can make peace. People must learn to love each other, and our organization, *Chefs for Peace*, makes a major contribution to society: through food to peace. For me, being a member of *Chefs for Peace* means a lot. I personally believe that peace is not only possible, but that all human beings must live in peace. Jeff Young, *The Catholic Foodie™*, shares that mission in his book *Around the Table with The Catholic Foodie: Middle Eastern Cuisine*. Through recipes and stories of food and faith, Jeff encourages and inspires families – indeed, all people – to cook good food and to find faith and peace together around the table. *Bil Hana Wishshifa… Bon appetit!*

Chef Nabil M. Aho,
Head Chef Instructor,
Professional Promotion Hospitality Section,
Notre Dame of Jerusalem Center

Jeff Young serves up a tantalizing blend of Middle Eastern food, faith, history, and travel. He turns the seemingly exotic tastes and flavors of the Holy Land into fabulous yet simple recipes that any Catholic foodie can recreate right at home.

Mary DeTurris Poust
Author of *Cravings: A Catholic Wrestles with Food, Self-Image, and God*

Jeff has a love for life and the wonderful things God has given us. It is not only contagious, but it resonates in everything he does, especially when he talks about food. So when you combine Jeff's passion for food with the mouth-watering foods of the Holy Land, well, it's a recipe for AWESOMENESS! One of my favorite places in the Holy Land is Cana, where Jesus performed his first miracle: turning water into wine at a wedding. For me, this miracle says so much about how God wants us to be happy and enjoy the yummy things in life, and it is this very perspective from which Jeff presents this delectable array of recipes. Reading this book is like having Jeff sit next to you in the kitchen, chit-chatting while he shows you how to make magic. If you've been to the Holy Land, it's a great way to remember all of the scrumptious foods you had when you were there; and if you haven't been, you'll want to go after you make just a few of these delectable recipes. Start with the pita, then add the hummus. Mix up a little fattoush, and I'll be right over!

Diane von Glahn
Host of *The Faithful Traveler*

What you hold in your hands is more than a cookbook, more than a collection of great food writing, more than a perspective on faith woven in with mealtime. Jeff Young has collected an approach to food, faith, and family that even the non-cooks among us will appreciate, savor, and enjoy.

Sarah Reinhard
Author and Blogger at *the Snoring Scholar*

The combination of a spiritual pilgrimage to the Holy Land with recipes from many of the local areas visited is a rare treat in a cookbook. It provides double flavor: spiritual food and tasty dishes.

Most Reverend Sam Jacobs
Bishop Emeritus of the Diocese of Houma–Thibodaux

Around the Table

We Have to Eat, Right?

I mean, generally speaking, we eat three times a day. We need food to stay alive. But eating isn't just about putting fuel in a machine. Not at all. If we put things in their proper context, we will see that food is really about meals, and meals are about communion.

God created us for communion. Communion with himself and communion with each other. In the deepest part of who we are as human beings, God planted a fundamental desire for communion. Each of us has that desire, and so does every other human being who has ever walked this planet.

When I was a seminarian studying theology, I remember a professor telling us everything we need to know about the meaning and purpose of life can be found in the first three chapters of Genesis. In those chapters we learn who God is, who we are, and what life is all about. Life is about relationship, it's about communion.

I grew up in south Louisiana, Baton Rouge to be specific, and I have lived in the Archdiocese of New Orleans now for almost 20 years. New Orleans is known the world over for jazz, Mardi Gras, and good food. It's also known for its Catholic roots. I guess you could say that writing about "food meets faith" was inevitable for me. From an early age I was surrounded by good food and good cooks. I was blessed to have a mother who stayed home, and she cooked dinner every night. We got together with extended family at my grandparents' house every Sunday for lunch. All the cousins and aunts and uncles were there, and the gathering centered around lunch. My grandparents were excellent cooks, by the way.

That's one thing about south Louisiana. There are so many cooks. Not just famous chefs—we have plenty of those too—I'm talking about regular people who, when they are not at their real jobs, thoroughly enjoy cooking. There's a "compliment" that waiters, waitresses and chefs hear from time to time in Louisiana. It's funny, but it conveys a point. When asked by a server or chef how the steak was, or the étouffée, or the Shrimp Creole, or whatever, the diner might say something along these lines, "Oh, it was great! It was almost as good as mine." It seems, around here, that everyone is a cook.

I started cooking when I was about 11. The first thing I think I ever made was my favorite food: pizza. But I made it from a box (either Chef Boyardee or an Appian Way pizza kit). Definitely not the best, but I learned enough from following the directions on the box to quickly move on to making my own dough and, eventually, my own sauce. I've never looked back.

When I was 18 I joined Blessed Mother Teresa's priests, the Missionaries of Charity Fathers. I was in formation with them in Tijuana, Mexico, for two years and I

loved it. That house of formation was made up of 50 guys from 12 different nations. Since we had school, ministry, and other duties during the week, we hired a cook to prepare our lunches and dinners from Monday to Friday. But on the weekends, we had rotating teams that were responsible for cooking our meals. Five teams rotated each weekend, and each team was led by a captain. There were two Italian team captains, one from Milan and the other from Venice. There was one French team captain, a joyful young man from Paris. There was a team captain from India. And then there was me. By virtue of the fact that if I was from Louisiana, I must know how to cook, right? It seems that's a common assumption about people from Louisiana. That, and the fact we all have alligators as pets in our backyards.

Good Things Happen Around the Table

I never made it to ordination. After four years in the seminary, I discerned that God had different plans for me. In 1998 I married the love of my life and I am now a husband and the father of three amazing children. But I learned a lot about family when I was in the seminary. All our meals were communal, so we were together around the table three times a day with—more or less—the same group of people. There were no televisions, and there was no radio blaring in the background. We talked. We conversed. And at some meals during Lent, a designated reader would read to us passages from spiritual books. At meals we nourished our bodies and our souls.

My wife's family is Lebanese, and she grew up in Baton Rouge too, with a big family and big family celebrations. And all those celebrations happened around food. Good food.

My wife and I both enjoy cooking, and we both recognize the importance of family meals. Early on in our marriage we decided to make mealtime, especially dinner, a priority. It's not easy, and it is getting tougher as our kids get older, but it is still a priority.

Dining together is something families everywhere struggle with. It seems that dining together is becoming a lost art. This is a relatively new concern in our society. For centuries (and even longer), removing food from the context of a meal wasn't much of an issue. Until the Industrial Revolution, most societies were agrarian. Everything centered around the cultivation and harvesting of food. Without electricity and other comforts of modern technology, the day was much shorter. The sun dictated everything. Women spent most of the day preparing the meals. It was an all-day affair. Men were out in the fields working, or building, or hunting. In essence, life was all about food. But food was always a communal event. A meal.

Today we are too busy for our own good. We are constantly on the run, and we eat on the run too. One of the major casualties of our hectic lifestyle is shared meals. From a purely natural standpoint, we can see this is not good. The results of eating on the run range from less time spent with loved ones to eating food that is just not healthy. But from a spiritual perspective, taking food out of the context of a meal has greater consequences. When we gather around the table for a meal, we share not only the food, but ourselves. Eating is a very intimate experience.

Sharing a meal brings people together, literally and figuratively. Think about it. First dates typically take place across the table in a restaurant. Wedding receptions feature food and drink. Gathering around the table is one of the few times in life we sit face-to-face with people and have the opportunity to really connect with them.

And here's the neat thing: God made us this way.

The Bible Is Full of Food

From Genesis to Revelation, food plays an important role in salvation history. And so has the table. In the Old Testament, every covenant God made with his people was sealed with a meal. And every covenant had the purpose of increasing the size of the family of God. The greatest Old Testament covenant provides the most striking example of this. In the Passover celebration God links the eating of a shared meal with the salvation of his people. It is no coincidence Jesus instituted the Eucharist within the context of a meal.

Maybe meals are so important to God because that's how sin entered the world. In the Exultet sung at the Easter Vigil, we hear the Fall referred to as the *felix culpa*, the happy fault, that merited for us so great a savior. Have you ever thought about the fact that the first sin occurred through an act of eating? Of course it was a sin of disobedience, a sin of pride. It was man and woman desiring to be like God, to replace God. But if you read the story as a story, you see that the sin was committed through an act of eating. Like all eating, it was an intimate act. Eve taking within herself the fruit, sharing it with her husband who was standing next to her. A shared meal. But it was the wrong kind of communion, and by it sin and death entered the world.

Pope Francis has a devotion to Our Lady as the "Undoer of Knots." This is a devotion he fostered and promoted in Argentina, a devotion that began around the year 1700. But the concept of undoing knots is very biblical. Specifically, the devotion harkens back to the early Church Father Saint Iraneus who referred to Mary's obedience undoing the knot of Eve's disobedience, but we can see other examples in the Scriptures. When the Israelites were wandering in the desert for 40 years, there was a time when they grumbled against Moses and against God, and God allowed seraph serpents to bite the people. Moses interceded for them, and God commanded Moses to fashion a bronze serpent and mount it on a pole. Anyone bitten by a serpent could look upon the bronze serpent and they would be saved. Just like he does with the cross, God always seems to save us by means of the very thing that is our downfall. He takes something evil and somehow turns it into good. And that is the very thing he did in instituting the Eucharist.

In the sixth chapter of John's Gospel we read the marvelous words: "He who eats my flesh and drinks my blood will have eternal life, and I will raise him on the last day." The act of eating is what brought sin and death into the world, but Jesus tells us in John's gospel that salvation will also come to us if we eat his flesh and drink his blood.

I firmly believe this is no accident. Jesus, like our Father (and like Our Lady!), is the great undoer of knots, and he undid sin and death using the very means by which they entered the world: eating.

The book of Revelation, in Chapter 19, gives us a sneak peek of what awaits us at the end of time: the wedding feast of the Lamb!

The Catholic Foodie…Where Food Meets Faith!

How Did The Catholic Foodie Come About?

I used to be a teacher. I taught Religion, Spanish, and Latin. And I have always been a geek. I like computers and gadgets, and I tend to be what social anthropologists call an early adopter. When it comes to technology, I like to be on the cutting edge. So it is no surprise that I picked up an iPod shortly after it made its debut, and I quickly jumped onboard with the new phenomenon of podcasting that followed in the wake of the iPod's release. I introduced this new technology into my classroom, recording lessons, coupling the audio with slides, and publishing them on iTunes as video podcasts for my Spanish students. I did the same thing in an audio format for the high school students I taught in my parish's Parish School of Religion and Confirmation Preparation programs. The kids loved it, saying it really helped them to study and to learn, and I was having a ball.

In October of 2008 I started thinking of launching another podcast, this time one that wasn't related to work. I wanted to do something fun, but also something I was passionate about. I kept going back to the topics of food and faith. Not only were those two things very important parts of my life, but I noticed they resonated with other people too. By the end of the month, I had registered the domain name *CatholicFoodie. com* and I had my tagline in mind: *Where food*

meets faith. Over the next couple of weeks, I built the web site and launched the first episode of *The Catholic Foodie* podcast, just in time for Thanksgiving. I had no real plans of where I wanted this thing to go. I was having fun, and people started listening. I was surprised to see the show quickly gained a following, and in the summer of 2009, I was invited to become an affiliate of the Star Quest Production Network (SQPN), a worldwide Catholic new media network of podcasters. The rest, as they say, is history.

The Catholic Foodie™ has come a long way since then. In addition to the web site and the podcast, I am now a co-host on a locally produced radio show called Around the Table, which is broadcasted in Baton Rouge and New Orleans on Friday afternoons. I am a frequent guest on radio shows around the country, talking about food and faith, and traffic on *CatholicFoodie.com* continues to increase. The recipes on the web site are a great resource, but my main goal is to inspire and encourage families to get back into the kitchen and around the table.

I see *The Catholic Foodie*™ as a door-opener, a greeter. I mentioned earlier that Revelation shows us that we are all headed toward the wedding feast of the Lamb. Mass, the Eucharist, is a foretaste of that eternal feast, and I see my job as the greeter. I open the door. I smile. I welcome newcomers and invite them to make themselves at home.

I do all of this by talking about "food meets faith." There's a rationale behind this phrase. As I said in the beginning of this introduction, we have to eat. But we also like to eat. Eating is pleasurable. And when we are not eating, we like to talk about food. Food is a wonderful place to start a conversation. And food dovetails so well with faith, it can be relatively easy to move from food to faith, from the common to the extraordinary. That's what I try to do at least.

The Middle Eastern Connection

I've already told you that my wife's family is Lebanese. When I was dating my wife, we spent a lot of time with her family, and there was always plenty of really good food around. When I say family, I'm talking extended family. There was always some occasion for all the cousins to get together. I think I fell in love with Lebanese cuisine at the same time I fell in love with my wife. It was a whole new world to me. I could cook Cajun and Creole, Italian, and Mexican, but Lebanese was foreign to me. It was exotic.

Over the years, I have learned so much about Middle Eastern cuisine from my mother-in-law and other members of the family. So when I received a call from Edita Krunic of Select International Tours in the spring of 2013 about possibly leading a pilgrimage to the Holy Land, I was intrigued. My first thought was how amazing it would be to eat some of the same foods that we cooked on a regular basis, but to eat them at their birthplace, so to speak. And then it hit me. The Holy Land was holy because of Jesus. He lived his life there. God became man there. Jesus lived, walked, talked, ate, instituted the sacraments, suffered, died, and rose from the dead there. Of course, I had to go! So in February 2014, the first ever "Food Meets Faith" pilgrimage to the Holy Land happened. It was an amazing experience, and this book you are reading is part of the fruit of that pilgrimage.

In addition to all of the traditional pilgrimage experiences in the Holy Land, we were treated to a deliciously foodie buffet of

events, including talks on biblical food and cooking demonstrations by the organization *Chefs for Peace*, which is comprised of Christian, Jewish, and Muslim chefs who strive to bring about peace through food. We also had a number of celebratory suppers, in addition to celebrating Mass at the holy sites each day. We grew in faith together around the table of the Eucharist and around the dinner table. It was the perfect "where food meets faith" event.

I learned something important on that trip. Going on pilgrimage isn't only about me growing in faith. That happens, of course. I do receive grace upon grace when visiting the holy places that commemorate the events in the life of Jesus. But those holy places aren't holy only because Jesus lived there. They are holy because he still lives there in the Christian people who call the Holy Land home. They are the Living Stones of the Church, and their population has decreased dramatically in recent years. Today in Bethlehem, which is in Palestine, the Christian population is down to less than 2 percent. In 1964, there were 30,000 Christians in the Old City of Jerusalem. Today there are fewer than 11,000. That is only 1.5 percent of the total population of 800,000 in the Old City. There is a very real concern that Jerusalem could become a museum, a spiritual "Disneyland," a great place for tourists and pilgrims, but not for the Arab Christians whose roots date back to the Church's very beginnings.

By going on pilgrimage to the Holy Land, I am able to form friendships with the Living Stones, the Arab Christians, who live there. By patronizing only Christian shops and tour companies, I support them and help them to maintain a Christian presence in the Holy Land.

At the end of February, I returned home from Israel exhausted, but determined to get back to the Holy Land as soon as possible, and to bring others with me. I wasn't home a week before plans were under way for my next Food Meets Faith pilgrimage to the Holy Land, which will be in February 2015. If the Lord wills it, I plan to go back at least once a year.

I am grateful to Select International and Voice of Faith Tours for their efforts in bringing to our awareness the plight of Christians in the Holy Land and for providing concrete ways for us to help them. One of those ways is through a program called *Select to Give*. Select to Give is nonprofit foundation that raises awareness of, and provides support to, the "living stones," the Christians in the Holy Land. The mission of Select to Give is to help the Christians of the Holy Land to stay and work in the land of their birth in safety and freedom. The foundation accomplishes this goal by matching pilgrim donations up to $50 per contribution and using those funds to provide economic support and educational opportunities, especially for disadvantaged families.

Another part of Select to Give is a program called "Sharing the Bread." This program brings together small groups of US pilgrims with Christian families in Bethlehem, enabling them to share a meal together on Sunday afternoons. This part of Select to Give really gets to the heart of it all: relationships. Friendships are formed around the table and pilgrims return home knowing in their hearts that the "Living Stones" of the Holy Land— people with names and faces—need our support and our prayers so that they can continue to be Jesus' living presence in the Holy Land.

Select International Tours is committed to supporting the Christian presence in the Holy Land through employment as well. Select strives to employ only Christian guides, bus drivers, and other service providers as much as possible. They also make the extra effort to take pilgrims to shops that are owned by Christians…all to help keep Christians in the Holy Land.

Who Is this Book for?

It's for you. It's for anyone who seeks to grow in faith around the table. It's for anyone seeking Catholic culinary inspiration to get into the kitchen and to gather with family and friends around the table.

My sincere prayer is that the stories and recipes in this book will inspire and encourage you to find God with you around the table of the Eucharist and around your family dinner table.

And don't be a stranger. I'd love to hear from you!

You can find me at *CatholicFoodie.com*.

bon appétit!

Before You Get Started:
Tips for Cooking Middle Eastern Food

- My favorite tool in the kitchen, after my chef's knife, is my mortar and pestle. Nine times out of ten, if a recipe calls for minced garlic, I crush it with my mortar and pestle instead. Add a little salt to the garlic to create friction and beat it to a pulp, literally. We make salad dressing just about every day, and they all start with garlic being crushed with the mortar and pestle.

- Dried chickpeas are better than canned, but it takes planning. They need to be rinsed, picked over to remove pebbles or other debris, then soaked in cold water overnight. The following day they need to be boiled until soft. Then you can use them for Hummus or any other recipe. The only exception is Falafel. For Falafel, you only soak the chickpeas, you do not boil them.

- Sometimes eggplant can be bitter. To reduce the bitterness, you can coat generously with salt and allow it to "sweat" in a colander. The eggplant will sweat out some of the liquid that can make it bitter. Just make sure to thoroughly rinse the eggplant before cooking with it to remove the excess salt. This process works, but it can be long, lasting two to three hours. A quicker alternative is to soak sliced eggplant in salt water for 15 to 30 minutes. This will also prevent the eggplant from absorbing any olive oil you are using to cook it with.

- There are many different brands of tahini on the market. We used Joyva for the longest time, but our new favorite brand since returning from the Holy Land is Al Wadi. It is available in Middle Eastern markets and online.

- Your food will only be good as the ingredients you use. I always try to buy the best ingredients I can afford, especially when it comes to fresh ingredients and certain kitchen staples, like extra virgin olive oil. There are many different brands, and I can't recommend just one. Here are a few things you will want to look for as you shop for olive oil: 1) Look for "cold pressed" on the label, 2) look for "extra virgin" on the label, 3) packaged in green glass to protect the oil from the damaging effects of sunlight, 4) look for a date stamp on the label. Unlike wine, olive oil does not improve with age.

- Fresh squeezed lemon juice is always best. The $5 I spent on a little wooden reamer is probably the best $5 I have ever spent. I use it every day, and I am constantly amazed at what a little fresh lemon juice can do to a recipe.

- The salt that I use most days is simple kosher salt. My wife prefers sea salt, so we use both. There are so many varieties of salt, and each one can add a different flavor to a dish. Experiment and see which salts you prefer.

A note about language and culture:

The Arabic language spoken by many cultures in the Middle East is a very old language. Many of the words translate into English with different spellings. That's why there are different spellings for so many different dishes. For example Tabbouleh could be spelled Tabouli, Taboule, or Tabouleh. Makloubeh could be spelled Maklouba, or Maqlooba. Editorially, I had to make a decision for _CatholicFoodie.com_ and for this book. I have attempted to maintain a consistency that meshes with the way I saw words spelled in the Holy Land. If you want to do further research on any of the recipes in this book, keep in mind that you might need to search for multiple spellings.

A note about the difference of American Middle Eastern cuisine versus Israeli Middle Eastern Cuisine:

Shibly Kando, who runs the Kando Store in Bethlehem and also helps Voice of Faith Tours, is someone I met on my first pilgrimage to the Holy Land and we quickly became friends. We keep in touch on Facebook and he frequently comments on food photos I post. More than once, as I was testing recipes for this book, Shibly noted how differently this or that dish looked than what he is accustomed to in the Holy Land. He was in the States a few weeks ago and I had the opportunity to sit down with him and talk about the book and some of the editorial decisions I had to make.

I finally came to the conclusion that the beauty of cooking at home is that you can make dishes the way you like them. If you like extra tomatoes in your Tabbouleh, then you can add them. I also observed a natural fusion between cuisines takes place over time. My wife's grandfather (originally from Lebanon) moved to Louisiana in the late 1800s. Over the next century, the Lebanese dishes that were part of their daily fare began to take on Louisiana overtones. The results of that fusion are what I was introduced to in the early 1990s when I first met my wife. Does that make the food that I prepare at home any less Middle Eastern? No. This is simply part of my in-law's experience as people of Lebanese descent living out their days in America. In many ways, my experience of Middle Eastern cuisine has been a fusion between Lebanese and Cajun/Creole cuisines.

Bread: The Staff of Life

Bread has been referred to as the staff of life, because bread has been seen as a life-giving necessity in cultures across the globe. It is a common staple of life. It's no wonder Jesus (who was born in *Bethlehem* which means *house of bread*) left us his Eucharistic presence—the ongoing memorial of his suffering, death, and resurrection—in the humble and common form of bread and wine.

The Middle East is made up of different countries, different peoples, and different religions and cultures. Their cuisine, however, is strikingly similar, despite the vast differences in religion. The region is home to Christians, Jews, and Muslims, but bread is common to all of them. Actually, for all three religions, bread is considered to be holy, a gift from God.

What we know in the United States as Pita is known by other names across the Middle East. As a matter of fact, *Pita* is a Greek name. It is also known in the States as *Arabic Bread* or *Syrian Bread*. In Arabic it is *Khubz*.

Claudia Roden, reknowned cookbook writer and cultural anthropologist, tells a story in *The New Book of Middle Eastern Food* that highlights the reverence the people of the Middle East have for bread. At a conference in Istanbul a foreign correspondent stuck a piece of bread under the leg of a wobbly table to steady it. While apparently not a big deal for the foreigner, all the Middle Easterners who saw this dashed forward to retrieve the bread and kiss it.

In many areas of the Middle East, the act of baking bread is accompanied by prayer. There are prayers before starting, when kneading, before baking, and of course giving thanks before eating.

Bread

Loaves of Bread in a Middle Eastern Market

Arabic Bread (Pita Bread)

There are many different types of "Pita" bread in the Middle East. Some are thick, and some are thin. Some form a pocket inside when they are baked (which makes them ideal for sandwiches), and some do not. Some are topped with herbs and spices, others are not. But some form of flatbread is served with just about every meal in the Middle East. The bread is used to sop up sauces or dips (like Hummus), but it is also used as an eating utensil to scoop up meat, rice, or vegetables. Some salads even have a flatbread as one of the main ingredients, like the well-known Fattoush salad.

Make Pita at Home: It's Easy & It's Better for You

It's certainly true that Pita is readily available in grocery stores around the United States. But, I want to challenge you to make your own at home. It's easy to do, doesn't require a huge time commitment, and it's healthier for you than store-bought Pita, which is always full of additives and preservatives. Make it at home, and you're making it healthy with just a few simple ingredients flour, water, salt, yeast, olive oil, and sugar.

Baking Arabic Bread requires a solid pre-heated surface in an oven that is durable and can retain heat well. Regular baking sheets will probably not do the trick. A thick baking stone can work, but my experience with putting cold (or even room temperature) materials onto a hot regular-sized baking stone has always yielded in a broken stone. For any serious home baking, I highly recommend The Baking Steel made by Stoughton Steel, Inc. I prefer using a Baking Steel over a baking stone for three main reasons:

As a ¼-inch piece of steel. It's not going to break.

Things cook much more quickly on steel. Steel's thermal conductivity is 18 times greater than that of ceramic, which is what baking stones are made of. Not only will breads (and pizzas!) cook more quickly on a Baking Steel, they will also result in the oven-spring and mild charring that we have come to expect from restaurant and bakery-quality ovens.

It absorbs and retains heat well. So when you open and close your oven repeatedly as you bake Arabic Breads in batches your oven is less likely to lose heat when the door is opened.

INGREDIENTS

- 3 cups all-purpose or bread flour (I prefer to use King Arthur Flour, but you can use whatever you like), you will also need extra flour for dusting, etc.
- 3 tablespoons of extra virgin olive oil
- 2 teaspoons of instant yeast
- 2 teaspoons of kosher salt or sea salt
- ½ teaspoon of sugar
- 1 cup of water, plus a little more as needed

INSTRUCTIONS

1. In a stand mixer with a dough hook (or a food processor fitted with a dough blade) combine the flour, olive oil, yeast, salt, and sugar. Turn the mixer or processor on medium-low and slowly add 1 cup of water. You are looking for the dough to form a ball that is slightly sticky. You might need to add a little more water to make this happen. Usually, I use 1 cup plus 1 to 2 ounces of water before the dough is the way I want it to be.

2. Now it's time to let the dough rise until it doubles in size. This will take between 1 to 2 hours. You can leave the dough in the mixing bowl or transfer it to a large glass mixing bowl. Cover the bowl with plastic wrap or a clean, heavy kitchen towel. Leave the bowl in a draft-free place for an hour or two.

3. When the dough is ready, pre-heat the oven to 400 degrees. If you plan to use a baking steel, pizza stone, or a heavy cookie sheet place it in the oven first to allow it to pre-heat too. Next, turn out the dough on a lightly floured surface and cut into 6 even pieces. Gently shape each piece into a ball. Then, one at a time, roll out each ball into a round about ¼ inch thick.

4. Place each round on a lightly floured surface and lightly dust the tops of the rounds with flour, then cover with plastic wrap or a kitchen towel and allow to rise an additional 20 minutes.

5. When you are ready to start baking the Pita, dampen your hands with a little water and pick up one of the rounds of dough, patting off the excess flour and slightly moistening the dough. Then place the round directly on the baking steel, pizza stone, or baking sheet. Repeat the process as room in the oven allows, then close the oven door and bake for 4 minutes. At the 4 minute mark, flip the Pita and bake for another 4 minutes. The Pita should then be puffed up and nicely browned. Remove the Pita from the oven with a pizza peel or a large spatula.

6. Repeat the process with the remaining rounds.

NOTE:
- This recipe makes 6 Pita breads.
- This bread is delicious right out of the oven, lightly brushed with melted butter. If you are serving it with a sauce or a dip, like Hummus, you do not need to brush it with butter.
- Pita keeps really well. It can be frozen in packs wrapped in aluminum foil, then reheated in the oven when you are ready to eat.
- I usually double this recipe and freeze what we do not eat right away.

Za'atar Bread

The first time I had Za'atar was at a small mom-and-pop-owned Lebanese grocery and deli on Margarita Island in Venezuela. It was 1998 and I was on my honeymoon. I'm sure my wife had had Za'atar before, but I had never heard of it. The couple who owned the deli spoke English very well. They also knew my wife's uncle. Small world. We had stumbled upon that grocery and deli our first day or two on the island, and we immediately felt at home. The Lebanese people are a tight-knit people. They are all about family. This couple was so excited to meet us—relatives of their friend (my wife's uncle)—that they wanted to treat us like family too. And family takes care of family.

They put together a "care package" for us to have at our condo and a cassette tape (old school, I know) of Lebanese music. That was so cool! Then, when they heard that we wanted to travel the island to explore, they introduced us to the man who became our personal taxi driver, Virgilio.

The couple introducing us to Virgilio was huge. It made all the difference on our trip. We spent Thanksgiving day on a secluded beach with Virgilio and his family, eating homemade sandwiches, drinking beer, and singing along with Virgilio as he played classic rock songs on his guitar, like American Pie, Free Bird, and selections from the Beatles and Simon & Garfunkel. We sang our hearts out.

Virgilio, the Lebanese couple, and Margarita Island have absolutely nothing to do with Za'atar Bread, except for the fact that I was introduced to Za'atar in that deli. But I think back to those friends and those times every time I eat Za'atar Bread. Food is like that, don't you think?

INGREDIENTS
All ingredients for Arabic Bread
  (see page 26)

½ cup Za'atar (a spice blend you can purchase, or make yourself, the recipe is below)

½ cup extra virgin olive oil

½ teaspoon of coarse kosher salt, or to taste

INSTRUCTIONS
1. In a medium mixing bowl, thoroughly mix together the Za'atar, salt, and the olive oil.
2. Make the bread just as you would Arabic Bread, except don't allow it to rise after it is shaped. Instead, once the round is shaped, add 1 tablespoon of Za'atar to the round. Use the back of a spoon to spread it evenly, making sure not to get too close to the edge. You want to leave about a ¼ inch of space around the edge.
3. Bake the round just as you would Arabic Bread, except you do not flip it over. Bake for about 5 to 6 minutes, or until it starts to turn golden brown.

NOTE:
If you would like to make your own Za'atar seasoning, you can do so easily. Just mix the following together in a glass mixing bowl. Of course, you can play around with the measurements to create the taste you prefer.
• 2 tablespoons ground sumac
• 3 tablespoons dried thyme
• 2 tablespoons toasted sesame seeds
• 1 teaspoon coarse ground kosher salt

Iraqi Bread

It's amazing to me what can be done with the simple ingredients of flour, salt, sugar, water, and yeast. I was excited to have the chance to visit an Iraqi bakery in Jerusalem's *Mahane Yehuda* market. The bakery was called *Hassan's Pitot*, and inside I found two ovens unlike anything I had ever seen before.

The ovens are called tannoor ovens; they have an open hole at the top and are cavernous inside. Hassan, the owner, describes them as being like "a mother's womb," which fits, since bread is the "staff of life." I had never seen this method of baking bread. Hassan first shaped the dough by hand. He then laid it on a "pillow," stretching it as necessary to make it round. Then, most amazingly, he took the pillow, reached his arm into the opening of the tannoor oven and slapped the pillow against the concave side wall of the oven. And the dough stuck. The cook time is short, only a few minutes, and there is no "flipping" the bread. Like the Baking Steel, the tannoor ovens cook both sides of the bread at the same time. Hassan's breads come out charred and bubbly with a little crunch on the outside, but soft and chewy on the inside. Perfection!

Hassan uses no yeast in his dough. Instead, he uses a starter leftover from the previous day's dough. He has been doing this since he made his first dough in 1985. That means his breads come from a continuous dough that is 29 years old! I don't know about you, but I don't have a 29-year-old starter at home. I use yeast every time I make bread.

INGREDIENTS

3¼ cups all-purpose flour, plus more for shaping the dough

2 teaspoons of active dry yeast

2 teaspoons coarse ground kosher salt

1½ cups of warm water

INSTRUCTIONS

1. In a medium bowl, thoroughly blend the flour, yeast, and salt. Add all the water and mix thoroughly. Turn out dough on a lightly floured surface and knead for 10 minutes. Alternatively, all ingredients can be added to the work bowl of a stand mixer and kneaded that way.
2. Place dough in a large glass mixing bowl and cover with plastic wrap or a kitchen towel. Allow it to rise at room temperature for about 2 hours or until it has more than doubled.
3. Flour a work surface and scrape the dough from the bowl. Divide it into 4 equal parts and shape them. For each portion, start with the right side of the dough and pull it toward the center; then do the same with the left, then the top, then the bottom. (The order doesn't actually matter; what you want is four folds.) Mold the dough into a neat circular mound and turn seam side down. The mounds should not be sticky; if they are, dust with more flour. Cover with a damp kitchen towel or plastic wrap and allow the dough to rest until soft, about 1 hour. Preheat the oven to 500 degrees. If you are using a Baking Steel, make sure that you position it in the oven before preheating. You want the Baking Steel to preheat for about an hour before use. Note: If you don't intend to use the dough right away, wrap the balls individually in plastic and refrigerate for up to 3 days. Return to room temperature by leaving them out on

the counter, covered in a damp cloth, for 2 to 3 hours before needed.

4. After the dough has rested for an hour, it's time to shape it and bake it. Traditionally, this type of bread is made in a concave outdoor oven. Here we are aiming for a larger, thinner, and more pliable version of Arabic Bread. Roll out the dough into a very thin round, about ⅛ of an inch. Dust a pizza peel with a little flour and gently transfer the round to the peel. Jiggle the peel back and forth to insure that the dough moves freely. Finally, launch the dough onto the Baking Steel or the baking stone and bake for 2 minutes. Use the peel to remove the round and flip it over. Place it back in the oven and bake for another minute or two. Remove from oven and wrap in a clean kitchen towel. If you prefer a crunchier bread, then place on a wire rack instead. Repeat this process with the remaining rounds.

NOTE: MAKING BREAD

When it comes to making dough, I prefer to use a method based on Jim Lahey's "no-knead pizza dough," which yields a bread with a greater depth of flavor that is fantastically tasty and complex. This slow-rise method allows for a greater development of the gluten strands, which results in dough that will be easier to stretch and shape. I use ½ teaspoon of yeast (instead of 2), and don't knead the dough. I combine all the ingredients in a large glass mixing bowl and mix with my hands, just to make sure that it is all incorporated. Then I cover the bowl with plastic wrap and allow it to rise at room temperature for about 18 hours. It always turns out beautifully.

Mezze

Mezze is distinctly Middle Eastern. In the United States we are accustomed to appetizers before the main course, something either small or large, something for one or something to be shared with the table. Regardless of how large or small it is, the appetizer seems to be a rushed affair. Mezze, on the other hand, is like a walk in the park with friends in the cool of the evening. Except that there are several *small plates* all laid out on the table containing different salads, Hummus, Baba Ghanoush, various Kibbehs and Falafel. There's usually wine on the table too. And Arak, a milky-white anise-flavored liqueur mixed with water and poured over ice. But here's the thing with the Mezze: there's no rush. It's time spent leisurely with family and friends, enjoying good food and good conversation. Like the Italians, spending hours around the table laughing, talking, and eating is the norm in the Middle East. It's a way of dining that this American likes very, very much.

Typical Mediterranean Mezze Plate

Hummus

Growing up I hated beans. It wasn't the taste, it was the texture. To me they seemed gritty. Thankfully, my palate has developed over the years and I now love all kinds of beans. Beans are good for you, good tasting, and full of good nutrition.

I first tried Hummus at the invitation of my wife, though she wasn't my wife at the time. I spent a lot of time at her parent's house when we were dating, and meals in that house were always a big deal. There were no excuses for not trying something new and different, so when asked, I tried the Hummus. It was love at first bite. The creaminess, the garlic, the bite from the cayenne and lemon, and, of course, smoothness of the olive oil. What was there not to love? I had no idea it was made out of beans, nor did I care. It was too delicious.

Served with warm Pita bread, this chickpea dip is a hit at any party, and it's found on just about every table in the Middle East. You can now find Hummus in most grocery stores, but I think it's always better when you make it yourself at home. First of all, you can make it the way you like it. Secondly, you control what goes into it. Always use the best ingredients. If you make it yourself, you won't have to worry about any nasty additives or preservatives.

We make Hummus at home at least a couple of times a week. Recently, my daughters gave their lemonade stand an upgrade. They turned it into a Hummus stand. Seriously. You can get homemade, fresh-squeezed strawberry lemonade, made-from-scratch sugar cookies, and pick up a container of homemade Hummus to take home… all right in front of my house! Oh, and they offer free samples of the Hummus. They are so innovative!

So come by my house and get your hummus. Or you can just make it in your own kitchen.

INGREDIENTS

2 cans of chickpeas, rinsed **OR** 30 ounces of dried beans that have been prepared beforehand (**see below**)

½ cup of tahini

juice of 1 whole lemon

¼ cup of extra virgin olive oil (to start)

¼ cup of water (to start)

3 or 4 cloves of garlic, peeled

1 teaspoon kosher salt, or to taste

¼ teaspoon Cayenne pepper, or to taste

Sumac, optional

INSTRUCTIONS

1. Put chickpeas, tahini, lemon juice, garlic, water, and olive oil in the work bowl of a food processor.
2. Process until it becomes the consistency of Hummus. You will probably need to add more olive oil or water. Just do so slowly. Olive oil will make the Hummus richer and creamier. The water helps to thin it out.
3. **Taste. Taste. Taste.** You don't want the Hummus too thick or too runny. Make it to your liking. Also, add as much salt and cayenne as you like. Just remember to do so slowly.
4. Place Hummus into a round flat dish. Drizzle with extra virgin olive oil and garnish with chopped parsley. I also like to sprinkle the top with cayenne for an extra kick.
5. Serve with hot Pita bread.

NOTE:

Preparing Dried Chickpeas for Hummus

If you would prefer to use dried beans over canned, then follow these simple directions for a 1 pound bag of dried chickpeas:

1. In a large glass bowl, soak the beans overnight. Make sure there is enough water to cover the beans by a couple of inches.
2. Drain the chickpeas and rinse. Add to a large stainless steel pot and cover again with water (twice the amount of water to beans). For a creamier hummus, add ½ teaspoon of baking soda to the water.
3. Bring to a boil, cover, and lower heat to a simmer. Continue to simmer until beans are softened, about an hour.
4. Remove from heat, strain, and allow to cool.
5. The chickpeas are now ready to use to make Hummus. Just keep in mind that you will only need 30 ounces of beans for this recipe of Hummus. With a 1 pound bag of dried beans, you will probably have some beans left over. You can use them to garnish your serving dish.

Baba Ghanoush

Eggplant wasn't really a friend of mine until recently. We became friends just last February in the Holy Land. I had always found eggplant to be too bitter, and sometimes it stung. So I stayed away from it. But it's hard to stay away from eggplant in the Holy Land. Eggplant is so plentiful, so abundant. It is also more often called *aubergine* in the Holy Land, which I think sounds so much better than *eggplant*.

I mentioned before that Hummus is on just about every table for every meal in the Middle East. Well, it is frequently accompanied by its cousin Baba Ghanoush. Baba Ghanoush is an eggplant dip, and the method for making it is very similar to the method of making Hummus. As a matter of fact, they both include many of the same ingredients such as tahini, lemon, olive oil, and garlic.

It's the roasting of the eggplants until their skins begin to char and blister that lends a smokey flavor to Baba Ghanoush. The recipe below details how to roast the eggplants in the oven, but you can also roast them on a grill, if you like.

Baba Ghanoush is popular in the United States, and it is probably one of the most well-recognized Middle Eastern dishes. It's most often served with warm Pita bread, but you can also serve it with slices of cucumber, carrot, or slivers of red, yellow, or orange bell peppers.

INGREDIENTS

3 medium eggplants

½ cup of tahini

Juice of 2 lemons

¼ cup of extra virgin olive oil

3 cloves of garlic, crushed

1 ¼ teaspoon of coarse ground kosher salt, or to taste

¼ teaspoon of cayenne, or to taste

½ cup of water

2 tablespoons chopped fresh parsley, as garnish

Sumac, as garnish

INSTRUCTIONS

1. Roast the eggplants: Preheat the oven to 500 degrees. Line a baking sheet with aluminum foil. Rinse eggplants well, then pierce them a few times with a sharp knife or a sharp fork (uniformly over the whole eggplant to prevent bursting), and place on the baking sheet. Roast in the oven, turning every 5 to 7 minutes until the skin blisters and begins to crack. Remove from oven, set aside, and allow to cool.

2. Once cool enough to handle, slice the eggplants in half lengthwise and scoop out the flesh with a spoon, transferring it to a strainer so that the eggplant will release its liquid.

3. Place the eggplant in a medium to large mixing bowl. Add the tahini, salt, garlic, lemon juice and mix well with a fork, mashing up any larger pieces of eggplant. Slowly add water, as necessary, to achieve desired consistency. *Alternatively, the eggplant and other ingredients can be placed in the work bowl of a food processor.*

4. Scoop the mixture into a round serving dish and create a well around the area of the dish. Fill the well with the olive oil, and garnish with fresh parsley and sumac. Serve with warm Arabic Bread.

Mutabal

Very much like Baba Ghanoush, Mutabal is actually a different dish. It's creamier and smoother because of the addition of yogurt.

I have to admit that including Mutabal here is tricky, mainly because the terms *Baba Ghanoush* and *Mutabal* are often used interchangeably here in the United States. As a matter of fact, there are places in the Middle East where it is common to add pomegranate molasses, tomatoes, and walnuts to Baba Ghanoush, whereas Mutabal is always a more simple dish. However, both begin with roasted eggplant, which gives each dish its distinctive smokiness.

The quantity and quality of the produce in the Holy Land astounded me. It's no wonder there is such a variety of dishes featuring the same ingredients. It's like each recipe is a riff off of a common theme… and they're all good. For example, we had lunch one day in Bethlehem at a restaurant called Abu Shanab, which means "the big mustache." This was a special lunch, and it was totally off the itinerary.

Our guide Arlette really bonded with our group, as we did with her. As a Catholic woman from Palestine, she was able to share so much more with us about the places we visited than just the facts. She knows these places "in her bones," so to speak. Her home parish is the Church of the Nativity in Bethlehem, for goodness sakes!

During the course of our days with Arlette, we learned a bit about her family. One day she mentioned she would love to introduce us to her brother because he is a chef and owns a very unique restaurant in Bethlehem specializing in grilled meats, and instead of knives, they use swords. Yes, swords. Abu Shanab is aptly named since Arlette's brother Jamal Kara'a dons a magnificent—and quite large—mustache! And they do use swords in the restaurant!

As part of the Mezze, I noticed a dish I did not recognize. To me, a guy from south Louisiana, it looked like fried oysters topped with olive oil and lemon juice. It wasn't, of course. It was eggplant. If I remember correctly, I was told by one of the waiters that they call that dish Baba Ghanoush too.

So whether your eggplant is fried, grilled, or roasted, as long as you have Middle Eastern ingredients on hand, such as tahini, yogurt, garlic, and lemon, you can make a delicious dish.

Baba Ghanoush? Mutabal? I'll take it either way. For the Mutabal, the tahini and yogurt make it creamy, while the garlic and lemon give it its bite. When I make it, I add a little cayenne too…because I'm from south Louisiana.

INGREDIENTS

2 medium eggplants

3 cloves of garlic, crushed

¼ cup tahini

¾ cup full-fat Greek yogurt or Labneh

Juice of 1 lemon

2 tablespoons extra virgin olive oil

Kosher salt, to taste

Paprika and freshly chopped parsley, as garnish

Tomato, chopped, as garnish (optional)

Full-fat Greek yogurt, as garnish (optional)

INSTRUCTIONS

1. Grill the eggplant whole, or roast in the oven at 500 degrees, until charred on the outside and very soft on the inside (see page 36 for Baba Ghanoush). Remove

from heat, set aside, and let cool.

2. Once cool enough to handle, peel the eggplants and place in a large mixing bowl. Add the garlic, tahini, yogurt, lemon juice, and salt. Alternatively, you can add the ingredients to the workbowl of a food processor.

3. Mix vigorously with a fork and transfer to a serving dish. Drizzle with the olive oil and garnish with paprika and chopped parsley.

4. Best served slightly chilled.

5. Garnish with chopped parsley (and tomato, optional), paprika, and a dollop of yogurt.

Labneh: Middle Eastern Yogurt Cheese

Tart and creamy, *Laban* is a thick Middle Eastern yogurt. We often mix it in a bowl with some lemon juice and a dash of salt (all to taste, of course), and use it as a dipping sauce for Kafta, grape leaves, Kibbeh, stuffed bell peppers or squash, and Falafel. It's also great on any kind of "Pita sandwich."

Labneh is a strained yogurt cheese that is made from *Laban*. It does take some time to make, but the process is very simple. Labneh is made from sheep's milk or cow's milk, and it goes very well with warm Pita bread, olive oil, and Za'atar. It is very common on the Middle Eastern breakfast table, and is delicious served with sliced tomatoes, cucumbers, and olives.

Labneh can be made plain, or with any of the following (individually or in combinations): oregano, basil, thyme, chives, mint, rosemary, parsley, garlic, paprika, toasted sesame seeds, red pepper flakes, and sumac.

INGREDIENTS
4 cups of Laban (you can also use full-fat Greek yogurt)

3 teaspoons of salt

INSTRUCTIONS
1. In a mixing bowl, combine the yogurt and salt together (the salt helps to draw out the whey).
2. Place a colander in a deep bowl. I use a colander with handles. The handles prevent the bottom of the colander from resting on the bottom of the bowl, and this is important. You will be draining the liquid from the yogurt and you do not want the bottom of the colander to sit in the drained-off liquid.
3. Line the colander with muslin or cheesecloth folded over four times. If you don't have cheesecloth or muslin to strain the yogurt, you can use unbleached coffee filters lining a fine sieve.
4. Pour the yogurt into the cloth. Gather up the ends of the cloth and tie it up tightly to cover the yogurt.
5. To ensure freshness, store in the refrigerator for 2 days. Periodically check to make sure the liquid is not touching the bottom of the colander. Feel free to discard the liquid from time to time.
6. After 2 days, remove the drained yogurt from the cloth, wrap it in paper towels and transfer it to a plate lined with paper towels. Return the yogurt to the refrigerator for another 2 days, periodically changing out the paper towels. The goal is to remove as much of the moisture as possible.
7. After the final 2 days, remove the drained yogurt from the refrigerator, pinch off enough to easily fit in the palm of your hand and roll into a ball. Do the same with the remaining yogurt/cheese.
8. Place the balls in airtight jars and cover with olive oil. Store in the refrigerator.

NOTE: COOKING WITH WHEY
The drained whey can be reserved and used in baking to replace liquids called for in the recipe. Just keep in mind that the whey is salted, so you might need to adjust the amount of salt called for in any given baking recipe.

Spicy Red Pepper and Walnut Dip

You might be asking yourself, "Another dip?" Yes, another one. I have already shared with you the recipes for four, and I still have two more to give you!

Dips are a big part of the Middle Eastern Mezze, probably because of the importance of bread. Remember, bread is served at every meal. But don't feel like you have to serve these dips with bread. All of them can be served with fresh sliced vegetables for dipping, like cucumbers, red bell peppers, carrots, and cauliflower.

There is one ingredient in this recipe that might be hard to come by, pomegranate molasses, which is used in many Middle Eastern dishes. You can find it in most Middle Eastern markets here in the states, and you can order it online.

Pomegranate molasses is tart and sweet, and has a fruity flavor that is very distinct. It is hard to replace this ingredient. Can you make this dip without it? I think so. I'm a firm believer in the importance of playing with your food. Recipes are more like guidelines than rules. Every recipe should be made according to taste. If you can't get your hands on pomegranate molasses, you could make your own with pomegranate juice, sugar, and lemon juice. Just cook it down slowly on the stove. Or you can try to mimic the flavors with honey and lemon juice. But that would be a trial-and-error kind of thing… based on your taste, of course.

Notice that I specifically recommend Panko bread crumbs. Panko is made from bread without crust, and it has virtually no taste of its own, which means it picks up the taste of whatever it is combined with. Toasting the walnuts gives this dip a toasty flavor. If you want to increase that flavor, you could lightly toast the Panko too.

INGREDIENTS

3 roasted red peppers (you can roast them yourself, or you can purchase them in a jar), drained and coarsely chopped

1 cup of Panko bread crumbs

½ cup walnut pieces, lightly toasted in butter on the stovetop

4 cloves of garlic, crushed into a paste with a mortar and pestle

½ teaspoon kosher salt

Juice of ½ to 1 lemon

1 tablespoon pomegranate molasses

½ teaspoon cumin, or more to taste

½ teaspoon crushed red pepper flakes, or more to taste

¾ cup extra virgin olive oil

INSTRUCTIONS

1. Toast the walnut pieces in butter over medium heat in a skillet.
2. Add the salt to the garlic in a mortar and pestle and beat until you have a paste of garlic.
3. Place everything but the olive oil in the workbowl of a food processor. Pulse and blend together until smooth. Remember to push down the build-up on the edges of the bowl so that the finished product will be as smooth as possible.
4. With the motor of the food processor running, slowly drizzle the olive oil into the workbowl in a steady stream. Once well incorporated, stop pulsing and taste. Adjust seasonings and pulse again briefly to incorporate.
5. Serve with toasted Arabic Bread (Pita).

NOTE: ROASTING YOUR OWN RED PEPPERS

Red peppers can be roasted directly over the flame of a gas stove or a grill, or they can be roasted under the broiler in the oven. I like to use my Baking Steel to roast peppers, because it allows me to roast them on both sides at the same time. When roasting peppers, the goal is to heat them until the skins blister and char. Once they blister, remove them from the heat source, place them in a bowl, and cover with plastic wrap. Let them sit for 15 minutes. Resting like this will soften the skins and make them easier to peel. After 15 minutes, peel the peppers, discarding the skins and seeds, and use according to the recipe.

Creamy Tahini Sauce

Tahini is a paste made from sesame seeds. It's a lot like peanut butter and has a nutty quality to it. Tahini is one of the main ingredients in Hummus, so I usually have plenty on hand in my kitchen. But I have to admit that this Tahini Sauce is not something I made often *before* my pilgrimage to the Holy Land. Now it is one of my go-to sauces, mainly because it goes so well with so many things.

I was really surprised how frequently this simple Tahini Sauce showed up on our tables in the Holy Land. It's the perfect accompaniment to Falafel, Shawarma, Kafta, and meat pies. In Jerusalem we stayed at the Pontifical Institute Notre Dame of Jerusalem Center, called Notre Dame Center or Notre Dame Hotel for short. As part of our *Food Meets Faith* pilgrimage, Select International Tours organized an instructional and participatory lunch for us at the culinary institute attached to the Notre Dame Center. The Head Chef Instructor, Chef Nabil M. Aho, a member of Chefs for Peace (which you can read more about on page 18) taught us how to make Falafel from scratch. This lunch was such a treat!

From putting together the spices and seasonings to heating the oil and learning how to use a Falafel scoop, to assembling our own Falafel sandwiches, this wasn't just a lunch. It was a celebration. You'll learn more about Falafel and Falafel sandwiches on (pages 176 and 178 respectively) but for now I want to share with you this recipe for Tahini Sauce. It was on the table at our lunch with Chef Nabil, and it definitely went in my sandwich. It's simple to make, and it's versatile.

Adding water to tahini makes it turn whitish. When you whip it together with a fork or a whisk, the water also makes the tahini fluffy. It lightens it up. The addition of the lemon gives this sauce its perfect tang, and the garlic adds a bite. If you don't use it all, you can cover it tightly and store in the fridge for a couple of days.

INGREDIENTS

½ cup of tahini

2 cloves of garlic, crushed

The juice of 1 to 2 lemons, or to taste

2 tablespoons of full-fat Greek yogurt

1 teaspoon of coarse kosher salt

Chopped parsley as garnish

Cold water

NOTE: SUBSTITUTIONS

In a pinch, when I haven't had any yogurt on hand, I have made this sauce by adding a little extra virgin olive oil…and maybe a little extra water. This sauce is versatile.

INSTRUCTIONS

1. In a medium mixing bowl, whisk together the tahini, the garlic, the lemon juice, the yogurt, and the salt.
2. Slowly add cold water until you achieve the desired consistency.
3. Whisk in chopped parsley as garnish.

Lamb-Stuffed Grape Leaves

Stuffed grape leaves are distinctly Middle Eastern. Sure, the Greeks have their dolmades, but that's just not the same. Dolmades are good. They're just different.

These little beauties are present at every major family event throughout the year. And they are little. We roll them tightly and compactly. They are like finger food.

Stuffed grape leaves carry a certain mystique. At family gatherings everyone looks forward to them with great anticipation, and it doesn't take long for the pot to empty. Stuffed grape leaves are tradition, and family and tradition go hand-in-hand.

My wife's family is from Lebanon. Her grandfather—affectionately called *Big Daddy* —came to the United States from Beirut on a ship when he was just a young teenager. Like many immigrants at that time, he understood that, in order to be successful in this new world—in this melting pot of the United States—he needed to blend in as much as possible. Immigrants in general try to hold on to their culture and customs while blending in, and the easiest things to hold on to are the foods, the music, and the language at home, which over time dwindles down to just some of the words. That's exactly what it is like in my wife's family. A pot of grape leaves is more than just a pot of grape leaves. It's a people, a culture, a connection to the larger family.

It works the same way with other traditional foods. Tabbouleh is more than just a salad. Hummus is more than just a dip. These foods are a connection with the past, they are an affirmation of who they are. Rolling grape leaves is a labor of love. You don't just roll a handful, or even a couple of dozen. If you are going to roll a pot of grape leaves, then you are going to go all out. We usually roll at least 60, but we've rolled over a 100 at a time before. Maybe that's why grape leaves are a perfect addition to any big family gathering.

The recipe I'm sharing with you is based on the one handed down to me from my mother-in-law Toni Nolan. I am including them as Mezze because that is what they are traditionally. However, we frequently serve them as sides or even as the main course.

INGREDIENTS

- 1 pound. ground lamb (you can substitute with beef)
- ½ cup (scant) raw long grain white rice
- Granulated garlic or fresh-pressed garlic
- Salt
- Cayenne pepper
- Juice of ½ a lemon
- 2 tablespoons butter, melted
- 2 small cans of petite diced tomatoes
- Lamb shoulder chops
- Chicken stock (32 oz.)
- About 60 or so grape leaves (enough to fill stew pot about ¾ full)

INSTRUCTIONS

1. Grape leaves: fresh is best, but jarred is okay. If fresh, you will need to wipe them gently with a damp paper towel on both sides. You will also want to cut the stem off where it meets the leaf. It is best to put the leaves in a freezer bag and stick them in the freezer overnight before use. Leaves need to soften (wilt), and thawing them out does the job nicely. You can roll them without softening them, but it is a more difficult task that way.

2. The Mahshi (or stuffing): In a large bowl mix the ground lamb, raw rice, and granulated garlic (we use fresh-pressed garlic), salt, cayenne pepper (all to taste), melted butter, lemon juice, and about half a can of tomatoes. Mix thoroughly with hands.

3. Line the bottom of the pot with the lamb shoulder chops. We use an All-Clad soup or stew pot.

4. Rolling the leaves: Lay the leaf flat on the table or counter. Take about a small finger's worth of mahshi and place it at the base of leaf (you do not want it to hang over the leaf). Fold the sides of the leaf in and then roll the leaf up to the top. Place leaf in pot on top of the lamb shoulder chops. Repeat the process until all mahshi is gone (or until there is no more room in the pot). Remember to alternate direction of leaves for each layer in the pot.

5. Add the remaining ingredients to the pot: chicken stock, can of tomatoes, lemon juice (we also add 3 cloves of sliced garlic). The liquid should just about cover the grape leaves (you can use more tomatoes, if desired).

6. Place a pottery plate on top of the leaves. This prevents the leaves from unrolling during cooking.

7. Simmer on low to medium heat for about 45 minutes.

8. Remove plate (carefully!) and serve.

Lamb-Stuffed Cabbage Rolls

I first tried stuffed grape leaves when I was dating my future wife back in early 90s. I think I tried them simply because I was fascinated with the woman I loved, and she told me they were good. Enough said. I do remember running an errand for my mother-in-law. Now this was years before she became my mother-in-law. At that time, she did not have her own grapevine, so she asked me to run and go pick some up from a family friend who did have a grapevine her backyard. It was the mother of a friend of mine, Father Jeff Bayhi. Well, a phone call was made, the leaves were packaged up, I was on my way, and Mama Bayhi was expecting me. The errand was a success.

Years later, my mother-in-law acquired her own grapevine. It was healthy and produced lots and lots of grape leaves for years. Then Hurricane Katrina stuck, and the vine was never the same after that. Eventually, that vine was uprooted and replace by a new vine. Fresh grape leaves are now plentiful in the spring and summer.

But what about the winter? Or whenever you can't get your hands on fresh grape leaves? I think that's why God created cabbage. Which is convenient, don't you think? In the south we have a custom for New Year's Day. I grew up with this, and since I hated beans growing up (and cabbage), New Year's never really thrilled me. But the custom is this: if you want to be healthy, wealthy, and wise in the New Year, you need to eat cabbage and black-eyed peas. Now that I'm older, that's not a problem. And, thankfully, the cabbage always comes in the form of Lamb-Stuffed Cabbage Rolls.

INGREDIENTS

1 pound. ground lamb

½ cup (scant) raw long grain white rice

Granulated garlic or fresh-pressed garlic

Salt

Cayenne pepper

Juice of ½ a lemon

2 tablespoons butter, melted

2 small cans of petite diced tomatoes

Chicken stock (32 oz.)

1 large head of cabbage

INSTRUCTIONS

1. For cabbage rolls, you need a larger head of cabbage. As you get toward the center of the cabbage, the leaves become too curly and are unusable, although you could use them to line the bottom of the pot. Cut the cabbage in half from top to bottom and remove the core. Parboil or steam the cabbage until the leaves are soft and pliable and are easy to separate. Larger leaves can be cut into triangles roughly the same size as a grape leaf. Remove and reserve large or coarse ribs. You will use some of the unusable leaves and ribs to line the bottom of the pot.

2. The Mahshi (or stuffing): In a large bowl mix the ground lamb, raw rice, and granulated garlic (we use fresh-pressed garlic), salt, cayenne pepper (all to taste), melted butter, lemon juice, and about half a can of tomatoes. Mix thoroughly with your hands.

3. Line the bottom of the pot with large cabbage leaves.

4. To roll the cabbage leaves: Cut the leaves uniformly until they are roughly the size of a grape leaf. I cut my into triangle shapes. Lay the leaf flat on table or counter. Take about a small finger's worth of mahshi and place it at the base of leaf (you do not want it to hang over the leaf). Fold the sides of the leaf in and then roll the leaf up to the top. Place leaf in pot on top of the lamb shoulder chops. Repeat the process until all mahshi is gone (or until there is no more room in the pot). Remember

to alternate direction of leaves for each layer in the pot.

5. Add the remaining ingredients to the pot: chicken stock, can of tomatoes, lemon juice (we also add 3 cloves of sliced garlic). The liquid should just about cover the cabbage rolls (you can use more tomatoes, if desired).

6. Place a pottery plate on top of the rolls. This prevents them from unrolling during cooking.

7. Simmer on low to medium heat for about 45 minutes.

8. Remove plate (carefully!) and serve.

Savory Pies

I've always loved Savory Pies. Growing up in Baton Rouge, Louisiana, I frequently enjoyed a Cajun cousin to these pies, the famous Natchitoches Meat Pies. Natchitoches (pronounced *NACK-uh-dish*) is a town in Louisiana that has become famous for its meat pies. You can get meat pies and crawfish pies in restaurants all over south Louisiana. You can even get them from street vendors in certain areas. And they are always available at spring and summer festivals from New Orleans to Lafayette.

Of course, the Middle Eastern flavors differ from the Cajun and Creole in many ways. Popular spices and seasonings from the Middle East include cinnamon, nutmeg, coriander, cumin, and cardamom, among others such as chili powder and even curry. They use cayenne in the Middle East too, just maybe not as much as we do down here in south Louisiana. It seems that many cultures have an easy-to-take-and-eat food. Whether the empanadas and tamales of South and Latin America, or the meat and seafood pies of south Louisiana, or the Savory Pies of the Middle East, these compact and portable "sandwiches" make the perfect street food and party food. It's no wonder they are so often included among the Mezze on Middle Eastern tables. And they are fun to make.

I make pizzas from scratch on a regular basis. I guess you can say that pizza-making is a passion of mine. It is something I am always trying to perfect, and my family and friends seem to be strangely thankful this is my passion. There's not much of a stretch between pizza, Arabic Bread, and Savory Pies. I make my Feta cheese, spinach, and meat pies on my Baking Steel, just like the Arabic Breads and pizzas that I make. Of course, you can use a baking stone or a heavy-bottomed cookie sheet to make these pies. In the end, whatever you use to make them, you will certainly enjoy them!

This recipe will yield approximately 60 3-inch pies.

INGREDIENTS

4 cups all-purpose or bread flour, plus extra flour for dusting, etc.

2 tablespoons of extra virgin olive oil

1 tablespoon of yeast

2 teaspoons of kosher salt or sea salt

1 teaspoon of sugar

1 ½ to 2 cups of warm water

Pie filling: see filling recipes for meat, cheese, and spinach pies on (pages 50–54)

INSTRUCTIONS

1. Proof the yeast by dissolving it in 1 cup of warm water together with the sugar. Stir to incorporate, then let it sit for about 15 minutes to activate. The mixture will begin to foam in the container.

2. In a stand mixer fitted with a dough hook (or a food processor fitted with a dough blade) combine the flour, olive oil, and salt. Make a well in the middle of the flour and pour in the yeast mixture, plus an additional ½ cup of warm water. Turn the mixer or processor on medium to medium-low, adding the final ½ cup of warm water only if necessary. What you are looking for is the dough to form a ball that is slightly sticky, but it shouldn't leave dough on your fingers when you touch it. You might need to add the final ½ cup of warm water to make this happen. But perhaps not. You don't want the dough to be too wet.

3. Let the dough rise until it doubles in size, about 1 ½ to 2 hours. You can leave the dough in the mixing bowl (or food processor bowl) or transfer it to a large glass mixing bowl. Either way, lightly coat the top of the dough with olive oil and

cover the bowl with plastic wrap or a clean, heavy kitchen towel. Leave the bowl in a draft-free place for an hour-and-a-half to two hours.

4. When the dough is ready, pre-heat the oven to 375 degrees.

5. Turn out the dough on a lightly floured surface and cut in half. Place one half back in the bowl and cover. Roll out the other half to about a 1/8-inch thickness. Cut the dough into 3-inch rounds, using as much of the dough as possible. Any leftover dough can be gathered and placed back into the bowl and used later to make more pies. Just remember to keep the dough covered, including the rounds you just cut. You can keep those covered with sheets of plastic wrap.

6. Working quickly, spoon a heaping tablespoon of filling onto the center of each of the rounds. To fold, grab the opposite sides of the round and bring them together over the center and pinch together. Then bring up the "back" part of the round and join it to the center too, pinching the rest of the edges closed. This method will yield a triangular pie. Repeat this process with the remaining rounds.

7. Place the pies on a baking sheet or a baking stone and generously brush each pie with olive oil. Place on the center rack of the oven and bake for about 20 minutes or until gold brown.

8. The pies can be served alongside Labneh (page 40) for dipping.

NOTE: MODIFYING YOUR PIES
- If the triangular shape is too much of a challenge, then you can go with the half-moon shape as an alternative. Simply spoon the filling more toward one side of the round without getting too close to the edge. Fold the round over the filling and use a fork to crimp the edges closed. This shape works well for meat pies.
- These Savory Pies freeze well, and they can be kept in the freezer for a couple of months (in plastic freezer bags, or wrapped in aluminum foil and stored in paper bags for freshness). They can be reheated in the oven without having to thaw first.

Feta Cheese Pies

This recipe makes enough filling for 20 pies.

INGREDIENTS

8 ounces of Feta cheese, crumbled

½ of a sweet yellow onion, diced

1 tablespoon of dried Za'atar

¼ cup of extra virgin olive oil

The juice of ½ a lemon, or more according to taste

INSTRUCTIONS

1. In a large bowl, combine all the ingredients and mix together with a fork (or by hand) until all the ingredients are thoroughly incorporated.

Spinach and Feta Pies

This recipe includes filling for 20 pies.

INGREDIENTS

1 pound of fresh spinach, chopped

¼ teaspoon of coarse ground kosher salt

1 medium sweet yellow onion

2 teaspoons of sumac

½ teaspoon of crushed red pepper flakes

2 ounces of Feta cheese, crumbled

¼ cup of extra virgin olive oil

The juice of 1 to 2 lemons, or to taste

Kosher salt and freshly ground black pepper, to taste

INSTRUCTIONS

1. In a medium bowl, combine the onions and the salt. Mix well with your hands, rubbing the salt into the onions. Let sit for about 10 minutes. The salt will cause the onion to sweat out its liquid.
2. Add the spinach to a large bowl. After the onions have softened, squeeze them by hand and add them to the spinach. Rub the onions and spinach together with your hands until the spinach begins to wilt and give up its water. Again, squeeze as much of the liquid out of the onions and spinach with your hands and transfer to a clean bowl.
3. Add the remaining ingredients and mix well with your hands until incorporated. Taste and adjust seasoning.

NOTE: DRAINING YOUR SPINACH

It's very important that you get out as much of the liquid as possible from the onions and spinach before sealing them in the pie dough. Too much moisture from the onions and spinach will dramatically impact the end result of your pies.

Meat-Filled Pies

Recipe makes filling for about 20 pies.

INGREDIENTS

Extra virgin olive oil to coat frying pan

1 pound of ground lamb

2 teaspoons of ground allspice

¼ teaspoon of ground nutmeg

¼ teaspoon of ground cinnamon

¼ teaspoon of ground cumin

¼ teaspoon of coarse kosher salt, or to taste

¼ teaspoon of freshly ground black pepper

¼ teaspoon of cayenne, or more to taste

1/8 teaspoon of ground cardamom

The juice of 1 lemon

2 teaspoons of pomegranate molasses

¼ cup of pine nuts, toasted

INSTRUCTIONS

1. Heat oil in a medium skillet over medium-high heat and sauté onion until soft, about 5 minutes. Remove from skillet and place in a medium bowl.
2. Brown the meat, but do not overcook it. Drain it in a colander, and then combine it with the onions.
3. Add spices and remaining ingredients.
4. Taste and adjust seasonings as desired.

Pickled Turnips and Other Pickles

Pickles are easy to make, and they are always present on the Middle Eastern table. I have never been a big fan of turnips, but these pickled turnips are delicious. They make a striking impression, too. Their hot pink color is not due to chemicals, rather it is due to the beets that are pickled right along with them.

It seemed that some kind of pickle accompanied every meal I had in the Holy Land, and I thoroughly enjoyed them all. Whether in a Pita sandwich or by themselves, the pickles I had were simple, crunchy, and tangy. Oh. So. Good! I have a hard time keeping pickles in the house, because my kids love them so much. Making them is much cheaper than buying them (just want to point that out, in case you have kids like mine).

Turnips aren't the only veggie you can pickle. Other delicious options include: tomatoes, okra, onions, garlic, cucumbers, asparagus, green beans, beets, cabbage, carrots, cauliflower, peppers of all kinds and colors, and more!

You will need 6 pint jars (or the equivalent) for this recipe.

INGREDIENTS

3 cups of water

1 cup white distilled vinegar

2 pounds of turnips, peeled and sliced into ½-inch thick wedges or into sticks

6 slices of a peeled beet

3 cloves of garlic, peeled and thinly sliced

1/3 cup of coarse ground kosher salt

1 bay leaf

INSTRUCTIONS

1. In a saucepan over medium-high heat, add 2 cups of water, the salt, and the bay leaf, stirring until the salt is dissolved.

2. Remove the saucepan from heat and allow to cool until it reaches room temperature. Once cool, add the vinegar and the remaining 2 cups of water.

3. Cut the turnips into 1/2-inch wedges or into sticks. If you cut them into sticks, make them about the size of French fries. Place 1 slice of beet into each jar (this is what will give the turnips their pink color), then divide the turnips and garlic slices among the jars. Pour the salted brine over the turnips, making sure they are completely covered.

4. Place the lids on the jars and let them sit at room temperature (in a cool place) for at least one week. Once done, they can be refrigerated until ready to serve. Pickles will keep for months when refrigerated. Top off with water if necessary

Salads

Lebanese Fattoush Salad, see page 54

Tabbouleh

This is one of those traditional family recipes that has a myriad of variations. Every house has its own way of making it. Some families prefer more bulgur wheat, others—like mine—prefer more tomato.

By definition Tabbouleh is a parsley salad. The Tabbouleh that I saw in the Holy Land was certainly heavier on the parsley than we are at home. Like I said, we like to add extra tomatoes. The only exception was Magdalena Restaurant. Sort of.

It was at Magdalena Restaurant in Migdal, overlooking the Sea of Galilee, that I was invited back into the kitchen by Chef Joseph Hanna to assist with the traditional preparation of Saint Peter's Fish for my group. My experience at Magdalena Restaurant, believe it or not, was one of the high points of the pilgrimage for me. Yes, the food was perfect and the presentation was impeccable. But that's not why it was a high point. At least, that's not the only reason. You see, food—as good as it can be—isn't really about the food. It's about the meal. And the meal isn't really about the meal. It's about relationships. Our group grew in faith and love around that table in Magdalena Restaurant. And so did I. But I also had the privilege of meeting new brothers, Joseph and Ahmed, who share my passion for food, faith, and family. And I got to cook alongside them.

Chef Joseph Hanna also happens to be of Lebanese descent, and his heritage comes across in his food. He makes local cuisine with a gourmet Arabic twist, pulling from the treasures of his heritage. You can find the same dishes throughout the Holy Land, but there is a distinct difference you'll notice in those same dishes at Magdalena. I recognized so many dishes, though, because we make them the same way at home.

INGREDIENTS

½ cup extra-virgin olive oil

1 to 2 bunches of fresh Italian flat-leaf parsley, finely chopped

2 to 4 tablespoons fresh mint, finely chopped

1 bunch green onions, finely chopped

1 sweet yellow onion, finely chopped

6-8 medium vine tomatoes, diced

¼ to ⅓ cup Bulgur wheat (preferably #1 grade, but you can use #2 grade), soaked in water for 20 to 30 minutes

The juice of 1 to 2 lemons

1 teaspoon Kosher salt, or to taste

½ to 1 teaspoon cayenne pepper, or to taste

Several of the inner leaves from a head of Romaine lettuce, washed and dried

INSTRUCTIONS

1. Once you have completed all your chopping and dicing and soaking, you can begin to assemble the Tabbouleh. I usually throw together all of the parsley, mint, onion, bulgur wheat, and green onion into a large glass salad bowl as I chop. I usually dice the tomatoes last and throw them in on top.

2. Add the ½ cup of extra-virgin olive oil and lemon juice to the bowl and mix well. It's best to go slow. This is one of those "you gotta eyeball it" recipes. There are lots of variables: the size of the bunches of parsley, the size of the bunch of green onions, etc. It takes practice (and lots of tasting!) to get it just right. So go slow on the olive oil and the lemon juice. Then season with salt and cayenne to taste.

3. Serve on plates, using the inner leaves of Romaine as a bowl for the Tabbouleh.

ABOUT BULGUR WHEAT

Bulgur wheat is used in many recipes in the Middle East, including Tabbouleh. Bulgur wheat is a whole wheat grain that has been cracked and parboiled and dried. It is sold in different grades, based upon size. For most of the Middle Eastern dishes that we cook, we prefer #1 grade, which is the finest grade. #2 grade works fine, and it is typically more readily available. In almost all recipes, the bulgur wheat needs to be soaked in water before being used. It doesn't have to soak for too long, usually just 20 to 30 minutes. Before using, we squeeze as much of the water out of it as possible by hand.

Lebanese Fattoush Salad

The Fattoush Salad is a classic Middle Eastern salad; and like most classic dishes, there are many variations on a common theme. Some families add purslane leaves or *mâche.* Other families might add Romaine or other types of lettuce. Coming from the same culture that gives us Tabbouleh, you will, naturally, also find parsley, mint, and green onions in this salad.

Whereas Tabbouleh contains bulgur wheat to give it greater substance, the unique element in the Fattoush salad is the addition of toasted Arabic Bread (or Pita bread). Lightly toasted and hand-torn, the bread gives this salad a crispness and a texture that is out of the ordinary yet very appealing. However, the inclusion of bread in this salad means that it must be served and enjoyed right away once the dressing is added. Otherwise, the bread will go soggy.

The Fattoush Salad that was served to us at Magdalena Restaurant in Migdal is one I will never forget. The presentation was impeccable, and the flavor most memorable. The fried strips of Pita on top were an absolute work of art. I'm looking forward to going back there soon!

For most of my life when I heard the word *sumac*, I thought of it in relation to poison sumac, kind of like poison ivy. But there is a variety of sumac (*staghorn sumac*) that is not poisonous. The berries of that particular sumac bush are ground and used in lots of Middle Eastern dishes. Sumac adds a distinctively tart bite that I really love.

In this particular Fattoush Salad recipe, I list the sumac as optional. If you can get your hands on it, I definitely recommend using it. But this salad is great even without it.

INGREDIENTS

2 loaves of Arabic Bread (or a thin version of Pita Bread)

1 bunch of parsley, finely chopped

1 bunch of green onions, finely chopped

1 bunch of fresh mint, finely chopped

1 cucumber, peeled and chopped

4 homegrown tomatoes, cut in small wedges

2 cloves of garlic, well crushed with a dash of kosher salt with a mortar and pestle

½ cup of extra virgin olive oil

Juice of 2 lemons

Kosher salt and freshly cracked black pepper, to taste

Ground sumac, to taste (optional)

Black olives for garnish (optional)

INSTRUCTIONS

1. Lightly toast the Pita bread, then break by hand into small pieces and set aside.
2. Finely chop the parsley, green onions, and mint. Chop the cucumber and cut the tomatoes into small wedges.
3. Toss the ingredients and mix well.
4. Add the extra virgin olive oil, the lemon juice and garlic. Then add salt and freshly cracked black pepper to taste.
5. Toss Pita bread in with the salad and mix well.
6. Sprinkle with ground sumac (*optional*)
7. Garnish with black olives (*optional*) and serve.

Spinach Salad

One of my favorite things to prepare for a hot summer's dinner is a salad. Cool crisp lettuces and fresh vegetables like tomatoes, cucumbers, and onions....So refreshing and delicious!

This spinach salad is one of our family favorites. The red onions, thinly sliced, add a mild bite to this tangy and creamy salad. Of course, the Kalamata olives contribute to the tang, along with the lemon juice and red wine vinegar. The olives also add salt, so be careful not to over-salt the salad. Finally, the Feta gives this salad its distinctive creaminess.

For an especially cool treat on a hot night, do this: prepare everything ahead of time, but don't toss the salad. Instead, place the salad bowl full of spinach, tomatoes, cucumbers and onions in the fridge for a while. Let it all chill, even the bowl. Remove from fridge and toss, adding the Feta and olives, right before serving.

INGREDIENTS

For the Dressing:

6 tablespoons of extra-virgin olive oil

2 tablespoons of fresh lemon juice

1 tablespoon of red wine vinegar

2 cloves of garlic, crushed

1 tablespoon chopped fresh oregano (or 1 teaspoon dried)

1 tablespoon chopped fresh parsley (or 1 teaspoon dried)

Salt, to taste

Freshly ground black pepper, to taste

For the Salad:

1 bunch of fresh baby spinach

2 large fresh tomatoes

½ of a red onion, sliced thinly

1 cucumber, peeled and chopped

¾ cup Kalamata olives

Feta cheese, crumbled

INSTRUCTIONS

1. Crush the garlic well. Use a little kosher or sea salt as an abrasive (I use a mortar & pestle to crush garlic).
2. In a glass bowl, whisk together the olive oil, lemon juice, red wine vinegar, garlic, oregano, and parsley until well blended. Add the salt and pepper to taste.
3. In a large salad bowl, add the spinach, tomatoes, cucumber, olives, and red onions. Add the dressing and toss.
4. Top with the crumbled Feta cheese and enjoy!

Tomato and Onion Salad with Mint

Simple and delicious, this easy-to-make salad was something I saw a lot of in the Holy Land.

We have been making a south Louisiana version of this salad for years, adding chopped cucumbers and red wine vinegar while dropping the mint. This is the kind of salad that says "summer" to us.

Nowadays you can get tomatoes year round, but this salad is always best when made with fresh tomatoes in season. Cherry tomatoes work best. Grape tomatoes are too small. Fresh regular tomatoes will work, but they will fall apart more when you toss the salad.

Experiment. Play around with this salad and try red onion instead of yellow, or add a little red or white wine vinegar in addition to the lemon juice. It's fun to try new things and to discover new tastes.

INGREDIENTS

2 pounds cherry tomatoes (or any other fresh tomato)

1 medium sweet yellow onion, cut in half lengthwise and thinly sliced

10 to 15 leaves of fresh mint, sliced

Juice of 1 lemon

2 tablespoons of extra virgin olive oil

Salt and freshly ground black pepper, to taste

Extra mint, as garnish

INSTRUCTIONS

1. Slice the tomatoes into bite-sized chunks. Some may only need to be sliced in half, others in thirds. No need to be "even" though. Think rustic.
2. Thinly slice the onion. If the bigger layers of onion are too big to be considered bite-sized, then feel free to cut those bigger layers in half.
3. The mint can certainly be chopped, but it makes a prettier salad if you slice the mint leaves chiffonade style. To chiffonade the mint leaves, simply stack uniformly several leaves on top of each other and roll them up tightly from the skinny point to the base. You will end up with a tiny "cylinder" of leaves. Hold the leaves together firmly with one hand while using the other hand to thinly slice the bundle. I can usually get 6 or 7 slices out of a bundle. This method will yield thin "ribbons" of mint that will add a bit of green beauty to this red salad. Be mindful of the fact that mint leaves are very tender, so you will need a sharp chef's knife.
4. Combine the tomatoes, onions, and mint in a salad bowl.
5. Add the olive oil, the lemon juice, and salt and pepper to taste. Mix well and adjust seasoning as necessary.

NOTE: CHILLED SALAD

This salad can be served right away, or it can be chilled in the refrigerator first. Chilling it first allows the flavors to marry, and it yields a very refreshing salad on hot summer days.

Palestinian Parsley Salad with Tahini Dressing

Growing up I always thought of parsley as garnish. It was that little sprig of green stuff they put on the side of your plate in restaurants. Protocol dictated that you ate your meal and pushed that little green thing onto the table so it didn't get in the way. Or was that just me?

Since this is a parsley salad, you would think it would be similar to Tabbouleh, but it's not. Both use parsley as a main ingredient, but the tahini dressing makes this salad very different from Tabbouleh.

This parsley salad is great served as an accompaniment to grilled or fried fish and meat dishes, or served as part of a Mezze.

INGREDIENTS

2 bunches of parsley, chopped (remove stems)

¾ cup of tahini

¼ cup of fresh lemon juice

2 cloves of garlic, crushed

Salt, to taste

Water, as needed

Diced tomatoes (when in season)

INSTRUCTIONS

1. Whisk together the tahini, lemon juice, garlic and salt in a mixing bowl until smooth. Add a tablespoon or two of cold water as needed to make a thick dressing. Adjust seasoning to taste.
2. Wash, rinse, and dry the parsley well. Remove the stems, and finely chop the parsley. Add it to the tahini mixture, and mix well.

Eggplant Salad

A number of years ago, when my kids were much younger (I think my youngest was about seven at the time), a farmer friend of ours gave us a couple of rabbits out of his deep freezer. I brought them home, thawed them out, and planned to braise them with beer. Guinness, I believe. If you do it right, rabbit can be quite delicious. I remember the whole meal was an elaborate production. We were so excited to try the rabbit. When it was finally done and we were all sitting around the table, after saying grace, we all dug in. Then there was a long moment of silence that was eventually broken by my youngest child saying, "Daddy, this isn't my favorite kind of chicken." It was dry. Very dry. And tough. It was hard to cut into, let alone chew. What I did not know when I started cooking that day was that my friend had given me some old rabbits. They weren't the young and tender ones. No. Not at all. Needless to say, those rabbits did not get eaten. Instead, I had to scramble to see what kind of sandwiches I could make for my hungry children. And what does rabbit have to do with Eggplant Salad? Nothing other than this: my youngest child's response to that rabbit has become a family "inside joke." Anytime any of us taste something we don't like, no matter what it is, our response is, "This isn't my favorite kind of chicken."

This may have been a rather circuitous way for me to tell you that eggplant wasn't my favorite kind of chicken for a long time. But that's the truth. I grew up as a very picky eater. It wasn't until I became an adult that my culinary horizons opened up. And my wife had a lot to do with that. I'm still growing. My palate is still developing. My culinary horizons are still opening up. I'm almost embarrassed to tell you that I didn't really start eating eggplant until last February when I was in the Holy Land. Eggplant was so prevalent, it was impossible to get away from it. So I ate it. And I discovered that I liked it. Funny world, huh?

INGREDIENTS

2 medium eggplants, sliced into ½ inch rounds

6 plum tomatoes (or 3 beefsteak tomatoes), chopped

2 red bell pepper, diced

3 cloves of garlic, crushed or minced

1 cup of parsley, chopped

1 cup of green onions (scallions), chopped

Salt and freshly ground black pepper to taste

Juice of 1 lemon (or more, to taste)

6 tablespoons of extra virgin olive oil

INSTRUCTIONS

1. Preheat oven to 375 degrees
2. Slice eggplant into ½ rounds, discarding the stem and bottom end, and place rounds in a large bowl of salt water for 10 to 15 minutes. The salt will help to pull out any bitterness in the eggplant, and the water will help to saturate the eggplant so it will roast well.
3. While waiting for the eggplant, chop and dice the rest of your ingredients and place them in a large salad bowl.
4. Rinse eggplant rounds under cold running water and transfer to a baking sheet, laying them out in a single layer. Brush each side with olive oil, then place in oven.
5. Bake for 20 to 25 minutes, turning only once at about the 15 minute mark.
6. Remove from oven and allow to thoroughly cool. When cool, slice each round into bite-sized pieces and add to the salad bowl.

7. Add olive oil, lemon juice, salt and pepper, and mix well.
8. Although this salad can be served immediately after mixing it together, I recommend letting it sit for a while so that the flavors can marry. If making ahead of time, you can cover the bowl with plastic wrap and place in the fridge for several hours.

NOTE: KEEPING YOUR EGGPLANTS FROM TASTING BITTER

As a general rule, when it comes to eggplants, the smaller the better. Smaller eggplants have fewer seeds and are less likely to be bitter. However, the primary factor in shopping for eggplants is firmness. You want a hard eggplant that is not bruised. Try to find the small firm ones. In a recipe like this, where you will slice the eggplant before roasting or sautéing, you can minimize the bitterness by salting it before cooking. Either soak it in a large bowl of salt water for 10 to 15 minutes, or if you have more time, you can generously salt the eggplant in a colander, toss, and allow it to sit over the sink and "sweat" for 30 minutes to an hour. If you choose the latter method, just make sure you rinse the eggplant under cold water to remove excess salt before cooking.

Cucumber and Yogurt Salad

First, let me start by saying that fat is good. Whenever I refer to yogurt, I am talking about full-fat plain yogurt, preferably, Greek or Laban. The flavor is in the fat.

There's a lot of misinformation out there about what is healthy and what is not when it comes to food. I prefer my food whole, or as whole as it can be. I do not want it broken down, deconstructed, filled with chemicals (or even replaced with chemicals)! No thank you. Give me real eggs, butter, cheese, milk, and yogurt, please. And real everything else too.

This cucumber and yogurt salad is another one of those salads that can easily be made ahead of time and refrigerated before serving. A little time in the fridge on a hot summer day can make a huge difference when served.

Cool, refreshing, and uncomplicated. That's how I would describe this salad. Toss in a little fresh chopped mint and you're on your way to being a celebrity chef to your family and friends.

INGREDIENTS

2 cloves of garlic, crushed

1 teaspoon salt, or to taste

2 tablespoons fresh mint, chopped, plus extra for garnish

½ to 1 quart full-fat Greek yogurt

2 cucumbers, cut lengthwise in half and then sliced in bite-sized half-rounds

INSTRUCTIONS

1. Place the cucumbers in a large glass mixing bowl.
2. Add the garlic, salt, and mint to the cucumbers.
3. Starting with about ¼ to ½ cup of yogurt, add yogurt to the cucumbers and stir to incorporate. Continue to add yogurt only until the cucumbers are sufficiently covered.
4. Serve, chilled, on plates, and garnish with fresh mint.

NOTE:

The amount of yogurt used is going to depend on the size of the cucumbers. It's best to start small with the yogurt, adding more as needed. The goal is to *lightly* cover the cucumber slices with yogurt.

Israeli Chopped Salad

Travel to the United States or the Holy Land and you will find that the Israeli Salad is as varied as the places you visit. Traditionally a chopped salad of tomatoes, cucumbers, and onions, some establishments (and homes!) transform this simple salad into a very impressive work of art. All of the chopping may sound like a lot of work, but it is totally worth it.

I like to make the dressing of olive oil and lemon juice separately in a jar, then toss it in with the salad. But you can certainly add the olive oil and lemon juice when you add the rest of the ingredients to the bowl, and toss.

If you prefer a salad with extra dressing, then refrain from seeding the tomatoes. I personally enjoy the juice from fresh tomatoes, and I find that it makes a great addition to this salad, even though it will make the dressing more "watery." In the Holy Land you will find this salad served as part of a Mezze, as a side dish, and even as a topping for Falafel or Shawarma sandwiches.

INGREDIENTS

3 medium cucumbers, seeded and chopped

4 medium ripe tomatoes, cored, seeded, and chopped

1 red bell pepper, seeded and chopped

1 large sweet yellow onion, finely chopped

3 cloves of garlic, minced

5 scallions, finely chopped

2 jalapeño peppers, seeded and minced

¼ cup cilantro, finely chopped

¼ cup parsley, finely chopped

¼ cup mint, finely chopped

½ cup extra virgin olive oil

The juice and zest of 3 lemons

2 teaspoons sumac

1 teaspoon cinnamon

Kosher salt and freshly cracked black pepper, to taste

INSTRUCTIONS

1. Mix all the ingredients in a large glass bowl. Cover with plastic wrap and allow to chill in refrigerator for at least 30 minutes before serving.

Israeli Breakfast Salad

Believe it or not, I love salad for breakfast. As a matter of fact, I'll let you in on a little secret. I frequently make "extra" salad for dinner so that I can save some to eat for breakfast the next morning! I know I'm not alone in liking salad for breakfast because it was available each morning in every hotel we stayed at in the Holy Land.

This Israeli Breakfast Salad is quick and easy to prepare. In the summer months, when tomatoes are in season, I like to top this salad with fresh chopped tomatoes and chopped mint.

INGREDIENTS

2 cucumbers, peeled

½ cup cottage cheese

½ cup feta cheese, crumbled

¼ cup sweet yellow onion, grated and drained

1 green bell pepper, seeded and finely chopped

¼ cup lemon juice

¼ cup extra virgin olive oil

Kosher salt and freshly cracked black pepper to taste

Fresh mint, as garnish

INSTRUCTIONS

1. Cut the cucumbers in half lengthwise and pierce in several places with a fork. Sprinkle with salt and let rest for about 30 minutes. The goal here is to pull out some of the moisture of the cucumber.
2. While the cucumbers rest, combine the cottage and Feta cheeses in a mixing bowl. Add the onion, bell pepper, lemon juice, and olive oil and mix together well. Season to taste with salt and black pepper.
3. Drain the cucumbers and cut into small cubes. Add to the mixing bowl and stir to incorporate.
4. Cover with plastic wrap and place in the refrigerator. Allow to cool in the refrigerator for about 30 minutes before serving.
5. Garnish with a sprig of mint, or chop the mint and sprinkle on top of individual servings.

Soups

Lamb and Vegetable Soup, see page 100

Chicken Stock

Chicken stock is an absolute necessity in our house. For years I bought cans of chicken stock at the grocery store. Then I discovered how easy and inexpensive it is to make a far better chicken stock right in my own kitchen. And the ones I make are not filled with preservatives, nor are they over-salted.

I keep several large resealable plastic bags in my freezer where I store bones and the remains of most of the produce I use in cooking. To this end, I rarely ever cook with boneless chicken. When I have the bones of two whole chickens, I know it's time to make a stock. All the ends of my onions, green onions, carrots, bell pepper cores and stems, parsley and cilantro stems, celery ends, and garlic skins and tips go into a separate plastic bag in the freezer. All for stock. And it is all so worth the effort!

There is one ingredient that I use for my chicken stocks that I did not list here: chicken feet. A couple of years ago, I read somewhere that chicken feet are excellent for making stock because they are high in collagen. They help the stock to gel when it is cooled. They also contain other nutrients and trace minerals that are really good for you. Shortly after reading this, I discovered a purveyor of chicken feet at my local farmers market. James raises pastured chickens and sells them at the market. It just so happens that he saves the feet and sells them too. The first time I bought a bag of feet from him (he sells them by the pound), I didn't know what to expect. My kids often help in the kitchen, and I was concerned they would freak out about the feet. But they didn't. After chasing each other around the house with chicken feet, they finally settled down and did what needed to be done. They have been helping me peel the feet ever since. That has become one of their jobs in the kitchen. Besides, they are better at it than me because their hands are smaller.

If you are able to get your hands on some chicken feet, just submerge each one in boiling water for 3 to 5 seconds. Remove from the pot and peel the membrane off. Cut off the talons at the closest knuckle, and toss the feet into the stock at the very beginning, along with all the other bones.

INGREDIENTS

2 Leftover roasted chicken carcasses (or the equivalent in chicken bones)... and put in *everything*....Don't throw any of it away!

3 yellow onions, quartered

3 carrots, well-scrubbed and cut in 2-inch chunks

1 head of garlic, cut in half horizontally

Leftover vegetable scraps (onion trimmings, garlic skins, parsley or cilantro stalks, celery stems and leaves)

2 Bay leaves

2 tablespoons of apple cider vinegar (we prefer the Bragg brand)

Filtered water

INSTRUCTIONS

1. In a large stainless steel stock pot, add the chicken carcasses and the apple cider vinegar, then cover with filtered water. Since I simmer my stocks for up to 24 hours, I fill my stock pot with as much water as possible without it spilling over when boiling.

2. Allow to sit for at least 30 minutes to an hour. This gives the vinegar a chance to work on the chicken bones. The vinegar softens the bones and allows more of the nutrients to escape into the stock.

3. Place the pot on the stove and bring it to a boil over high heat. Allow it to come to a full rolling boil.

4. Add the onions, carrots, garlic, and the leftover vegetable scraps.
5. Partially cover the stock pot with the lid and reduce heat to low and allow to simmer.
6. Simmer on low for 24 hours, adding water as needed.
7. Strain the stock well and cool. If you store it in the fridge the stock may gel nicely, but gelling is not necessary. You now have a nutrient-rich stock. You can use it right away, or you can store it in mason jars in the fridge, or in resealable plastic bags in the freezer.

NOTE:

I recommend stainless steel when making stocks or soups. In my experience, aluminum gives off a funny metallic taste.

Beef or Lamb Stock

Beef stock is always a treat. This stock comes out deep, rich, and dark, almost like coffee. It is nutrient-dense, and it is so good and delicious.

My stock pots regularly bubble with chicken stock from chicken bones, but when I have a chance to make a beef stock I just can't pass it up! It doesn't happen often. Luckily, I've been able to "stock" up on beef bones once or twice a year for the last few years. I make big batches of this beef stock, then store it in plastic resealable bags in the freezer. It doesn't take long to thaw out a gallon of stock to use in one of many delicious recipes. It is excellent as a substitute for lamb stock in dishes like Lamb Stew and Lamb and Vegetable Soup.

INGREDIENTS

Several pounds of beef bones (*6 or 7 pounds of bones....up to 10 if you have a big enough pot*)

3 Yellow onions, quartered

4 carrots, well-scrubbed, unpeeled, and cut in 2-inch chunks

2 celery stalks, cut in 20inch chunks

1 head of garlic, cut in half horizontally

Leftover vegetable scraps (onion trimmings, garlic skins, parsley or cilantro stalks, celery leaves)

2 Bay leaves

2 tablespoon of apple cider vinegar (we prefer the Bragg brand)

Filtered water

INSTRUCTIONS

1. In a large stainless steel stock pot, add the beef bones and the apple cider vinegar, then cover with filtered water.
2. Allow to sit for at least an hour. This gives the vinegar a chance to work on the bones. The vinegar softens the bones and allows more of the nutrients to escape into the stock.
3. Place the pot on the stove and bring it to a boil over high heat. Allow it to come to a full rolling boil.
4. Partially cover the pot with the lid and reduce heat to low.
5. Cook on low for 24 hours or longer, adding water as needed.
6. Strain the stock well and cool. If you store it in the fridge the stock may gel nicely, but gelling is not necessary. You now have a nutrient-rich stock. You can use it right away, or you can store it in Mason jars in the fridge, or in resealable plastic bags if you want to store the stock in the freezer.

Spinach and Lentil Soup

Lentils are a staple in the Middle East. As a matter of fact, biblical scholars believe that Esau sold his birthright to his younger brother Jacob for a bowl of lentil soup. Jacob must have been a great cook!

One of our favorite lentil dishes to make at home is *Mujadra* (a Lebanese lentils and rice dish), which we usually make at least once a week on a night when the kids have activities, and we don't have much time to cook. This Spinach and Lentil Soup is another go-to meal on busy weeknights. In addition to being super-tasty, Lentils are quick and super-easy to prepare. Unlike most dried beans, lentils do not need to be soaked or pre-boiled. They just need to be picked over (for stones and debris), rinsed, and then cooked for about 30 minutes. Easy, right? I first posted this recipe for Spinach and Lentil Soup on my website CatholicFoodie.com over a year ago. Since posting it, it has become one of the most popular recipes on the site.

We are a soup family. We love soup. Maybe that's because we are from south Louisiana where we grew up eating gumbo. I don't know. But I do know that whenever I make soup, I tend to make big soups. First of all, I am cooking for five people. Secondly, if I am going to expend the time and energy to make a soup (or any meal, really), then I'm going to make enough to cover at least two meals. There are exceptions, of course. But life is so busy that we don't always have time to cook. One way around that is to "batch cook" or to double recipes. My soup recipes are already big. If you are not a fan of leftovers, or if you want to serve a soup as an appetizer, then you could always halve my recipes for soups.

INGREDIENTS

3 tablespoons regular olive oil, not extra virgin (or you can substitute coconut oil)

2 large onions, finely chopped

5 cloves garlic, minced

2 teaspoons ground cumin

1 teaspoon cayenne pepper

2 cups red or brown lentils, picked over and rinsed

10 cups water (see note next page)

¼ cup fresh mint, chopped

1 bunch fresh spinach, washed (about 2 cups)

Zest of 1 lemon

Juice of 1 lemon

Kosher salt and freshly cracked black pepper, to taste

Laban or full-fat Greek-style yogurt

INSTRUCTIONS

1. In large stainless steel pot, sauté the onions in the olive oil (or organic coconut oil) over medium-high heat until they start to soften. About 3 minutes. Turn heat down to medium-low and continue to cook until they start to caramelize, about another 3 to 4 minutes.

2. Stir in garlic and cook for 2 minutes, stirring frequently to prevent the garlic from burning.

3. Add the cumin and cayenne, and stir to mix in well.

4. Add lentils and water. Increase heat to high and bring to a boil.

5. Once the soup starts to boil, reduce heat to medium or medium-low and allow to simmer until lentils are soft. About 30 minutes.

6. Add mint, and then add salt and pepper to taste.

7. If you want a creamier soup, you can mash some of the lentils against the side of the pot with a large stainless steel spoon once they are softened. Stir well.

8. Once the lentils have attained their desired softness and you are ready to serve, add the spinach. You can chop the spinach, if desired, but it is not necessary. I prefer to add the leaves whole. Spinach shrinks when it is cooked, so chopping isn't really necessary.
9. Add the lemon zest and juice. Taste and tweak with salt and pepper.
10. Serve in bowls and garnish with dollop of Laban or Greek style yogurt.

NOTE: USE WATER INSTEAD OF STOCK
Normally, when making soups, I advocate using stocks instead of water (usually chicken stock). However, I am amazed at how much flavor these little lentils pack. I prefer to use plain water when making soups with beans.

Lentils and Rice Soup

Another quick and super-easy lentil soup recipe is this Lentil and Rice Soup, which is also a very popular recipe at *CatholicFoodie.com*.

What is it about lentils? They are tiny little things, but they really do pack a punch, both in flavor and in nutrition.

- Lentils are an excellent source of fiber.
- Lentils are heart-healthy. They are known for lowering cholesterol.
- Lentils are full of B-vitamins and protein.
- Lentils stabilize blood sugar levels.
- Lentils are an excellent source of Iron.

The sautéed onions and olive oil, along with the lentils as they cook down, give this soup a creamy quality, although there is no cream in it. I like to top it with Arabic Seven Spice, but that is optional. Seven Spice can be hard to come by. It's available in most Middle Eastern markets and online.

Arabic Seven Spice is a blend of seven spices (cinnamon and cardamom are two of them) that yield a slightly spiced taste to dishes. It is also beautifully aromatic. If you can't find it in stores, you can get it online, or you can substitute allspice.

INGREDIENTS

2 cups dried red lentils

16 cups of water

½ cup uncooked brown rice

2 large sweet yellow onions, chopped

½ to ¾ olive oil (for sautéing the onion)

Kosher salt and freshly cracked black pepper, to taste

Cayenne, to taste (optional)

Arabic Seven Spice, to taste (optional)

INSTRUCTIONS

1. In a large heavy-bottomed stainless steel soup pot, bring water to a boil.
2. Rinse and drain the lentils, then add them to the boiling water. Reduce heat to medium-high and cook for 15 minutes.
3. In the meantime, sauté the onions in the olive oil over medium to medium-high heat, stirring regularly. Season the onions with salt and black pepper.
4. At the 15 minute mark, add the rice to the lentils and water. Allow to cook for about 20 minutes (though you may need to turn down the heat to medium, or even medium-low, toward the end of the 20 minutes).
5. Shortly after adding the rice, as soon as the onions have softened and become translucent, add them to the soup pot along with any residual olive oil. Taste soup for seasoning and add salt and black pepper as necessary.
6. Cook until tender (usually about 20 minutes).
7. Serve in bowls and season (optional) with a dash of cayenne and a few dashes of Seven Spice.

Lamb and Tomato Stew
with Crispy Potatoes

One of our first nights in Jerusalem, Select International Tours and Voice of Faith Tours organized a celebratory meal for our group at a restaurant in Bethlehem called The Grotto. The restaurant was next door to Shepherds Field, the place where the angels appeared to the shepherds to announce to them the good news of Jesus' birth. Dinner was preceded by a short presentation and cooking demonstration by the organization Chefs for Peace. Chefs for Peace is a non-profit, non-political organization. founded in the Holy City of Jerusalem in November 2001 by a group of Jewish, Christian, and Muslim chefs committed to working for peace through food. Chefs for Peace understands food—its preparation, sharing, and enjoyment—as a powerful means of creating a bond with others and revealing that which is valued by all three faiths: food, family, and friends. The organization understands the power of food as a bridge to mutual acceptance. I was blessed to meet some of the Chefs for Peace: Chef Nabil M. Aho, Chef George Alemian, and Chef Moshe Basson. I was honored to have been invited to cook alongside them.

That night we prepared lamb stew. We demonstrated the recipe using a single-serving, large clay pot. I don't recall the portions, but lamb (not boneless) went into the pot, along with a few different vegetables: onion, garlic, potatoes, carrots. After the vegetables were chopped and added to the pot, we added seasonings (salt, pepper, cumin, cinnamon, and allspice), and filled the pot with lamb stock. Finally, Chef Nabil placed an uncooked round of Arabic Bread on top of the pot to seal it. With that, the demonstration was over, everyone applauded, and we proceeded to the tables for the Mezze. What we did not know was that the chefs had prepared a single-serving pot for each of us. This was a big meal! After the Mezze, and some wine, the lamb stew was brought out, each of them topped with Arabic Bread. It was quite a sight! The recipe below is my version of lamb stew. I don't have a collection of single-serving clay pots in my kitchen, so I just use one big pot. I made a few other changes too. I use Kafta instead of bone-in lamb, and I roast my potatoes before adding them to the stew.

INGREDIENTS

2 pounds prepared Kafta (lamb meatballs). You can also substitute beef.—(see page 148)

2 to 3 pounds. Yellow Yukon Gold potatoes

4 tablespoons olive oil (for the potatoes)

3 teaspoons of salt (for the potatoes)

2 28 oz. cans petite diced tomatoes

2 cups of chicken stock

2 large onions, chopped

¼ cup regular olive oil

Coarse ground kosher salt, to taste

½ tsp black pepper

1 teaspoon cinnamon

1 teaspoon allspice

1 cup chopped parsley, as garnish

INSTRUCTIONS

1. Preheat the oven to 450 degrees
2. Make the Kafta (page 148) and shape into meatballs. Brown them in olive oil over medium to medium-high heat, then set them aside.
3. Par-boil the potatoes. To do so, thoroughly wash them and cut them into 1/2-inch thick rounds. Place them in a large pot and cover with cold water, making sure that the potatoes are covered by at least

an inch. Add 1 teaspoon of salt to the pot and bring to a boil over high heat. Once they come to a boil, you may need to turn the heat down a little bit, but allow them to boil for about 5 minutes. You don't want the potatoes to fully cook. You are only looking to parboil the potatoes and to draw out some of the starch and sugar of the potatoes.

4. Drain the potatoes and transfer them to a large mixing bowl. Working quickly, add 2 tablespoons of olive oil and ½ teaspoon of salt, and mix together well using a rubber spatula. After mixing well, add another 2 tablespoons of olive oil and another ½ teaspoon of salt. Once the potatoes start to look and feel pasty on the outside transfer them to a large baking sheet, laying them out in a single layer. Use two baking sheets if necessary.

5. Place on the lowest racks in the oven and bake at 450 degrees for about 20 minutes.

6. Once the potatoes are crispy on the bottom, remove the baking sheets from the oven and carefully flip the potatoes. Return baking sheets to the oven and continue to bake for another 10 to 15 minutes. Remove from oven and transfer the potatoes to a cooling rack. Once the potatoes are cool, cut them into quarters and set aside.

7. Pan-fry the onions in a little oil over medium to medium-high heat until they are soft and translucent. Add the petite diced tomatoes and the chicken stock, as well as the spices. Reduce heat to medium or medium-low and simmer gently for 30 minutes.

8. Add the browned meatballs and the potatoes to the pot and continue to simmer for another 20 minutes.

9. Serve in bowls and garnish with chopped parsley.

10. Rice Pilaf (page 114) is the traditional accompaniment to this stew.

NOTE: PARBOILED POTATOES

The process of parboiling the potatoes is what leads to the crispness of the final product. Parboiling draws out some of the starch and sugar from the potatoes, which ensures that they will crisp when roasted in the oven. I cut them into rounds because that is the only way to ensure even cooking of the potatoes. Once the roasted potatoes are added to the stew, they will soak up a lot of the extra liquid, making the stew thicker without losing any flavor.

Curry Chicken and Coconut Soup with Rice

I have already mentioned that my family is big on soup. That's one of the reasons I make so much stock. Sometimes, when it comes to chicken, it becomes a self-perpetuating cycle. Roasted chickens lead to stock that leads to more roasted chickens to make soup, which leaves me with more bones to make stock... And on, and on it goes.

This particular chicken soup recipe started out as an Asian soup. It was a family favorite I used to make every week. Then one day I discovered I could turn it into a Middle Eastern soup just by changing some of the seasonings. Reading through the recipes in this book, you will notice there is a "seasoning profile" that can be called Middle Eastern. Some of the more prevalent spices and seasonings in the Middle East include: cumin, nutmeg, cardamom, turmeric, sumac, caraway, cinnamon, allspice, saffron, coriander, fenugreek, cloves, and even curry.

This is another big soup. I usually make enough to cover at least two meals. You can make a smaller soup by simply halving the recipe.

INGREDIENTS

16 cups of chicken stock

3 jalapeño peppers, seeded and finely chopped

6-8 cloves of garlic, finely chopped

3 tablespoons of freshly grated ginger (or more to taste)

2 teaspoons grated lemon zest

2 teaspoons grated lime zest

The juice of 1 lemon (or 1 lime)

2 tablespoons spicy yellow curry powder

1 tablespoon cumin

2 teaspoons allspice

2 teaspoons sumac

Kosher salt and freshly cracked black pepper, to taste

2 cups of either sliced Shiitake mushrooms or crimini mushrooms, stems included

2 – 3 cups fresh green beans, cut

8 boneless chicken thighs, cut into chunks

28 oz. of coconut milk (2 14 oz. cans)

2 – 3 tablespoons cilantro, chopped

2 cups long grain rice, cooked to package directions in a separate pot or rice cooker

Sriracha sauce (A.K.A. "Rooster Sauce"), to taste

1 bunch green onions, chopped (to be added to individual bowls when served)

INSTRUCTIONS

1. Combine stock, jalapeño peppers, garlic, ginger, lemon zest, lime zest, lemon juice, curry powder, cumin, allspice, and sumac in a stockpot. Season with salt.
2. Prepare rice according to package directions.
3. Bring soup to a simmer and add the green beans, the mushrooms, and the coconut milk.
4. Season chicken thighs with salt on both sides and quickly pan fry in bacon grease (or some other oil with a high smoke point, like coconut oil or vegetable oil) on medium heat. Remove chicken from pan, and cut into chunks, then add to the soup. Alternatively, I sometimes roast chickens and add them to the soup.
5. Allow the soup to continue to simmer for an additional 3 to 5 minutes. You want to ensure that the chicken is fully cooked.

6. Add chopped cilantro.
7. Add Sriracha sauce, to taste.
8. Spoon about ¼ cup of cooked rice into each bowl.

9. Ladle soup into the bowls and top with green onions. You can also top with additional cilantro, ginger, and/ or more Sriracha.

Pumpkin Soup with Kale and Kafta

We are fortunate to have a very active farmers market right down the street from us. We are there just about every Saturday morning picking up whatever is fresh and in season. The farmers market is a happening place. People like to go there just to hang out. There's live music every week, as well as a featured chef doing cooking demonstrations and giving out samples.

A couple of years ago, the chefs from one of my favorite local restaurants were at the market giving out samples (and copies of the recipe!) of their Pumpkin Soup with Kale and Italian Sausage. David and Torre Solazzo are the married chef team behind Ristorante Del Porto. I think it's pretty cool that the restaurant is owned and operated by two chefs who happened to be married. To each other. There are two chef-couples that I know of in my town, the other couple are friends of mine, Keith and Nealy Frentz of LOLA Restaurant. You'll hear more about them later.

Anyway, I loved the pumpkin soup that Chefs David and Torre served that day at the farmers market. I took a copy of the recipe and I made it a couple of weeks later for Christmas. Like most recipes, I just couldn't leave this one alone. I play with recipes all the time. Change things around. Try different measurements. Swap out ingredients. Sometimes I do this out of necessity since I can only cook what I have on hand. But sometimes I do it just for fun. This one I played with for fun.

I swapped out Italian sausage for Kafta (lamb meatballs) and switched the seasoning from Italian to Middle Eastern. It turned out beautifully.

Try it yourself and let me know how it turns out.

INGREDIENTS

2 medium yellow onions, diced

4 ribs of celery, diced

1 med pumpkin, cleaned, peeled, and cut into 2-3 inch pieces

2 tablespoons garlic, chopped

1 gallon chicken stock

1 batch of Kafta (lamb meatballs... see page 148), browned

1-2 heads of kale, cleaned and chopped into 2 inch pieces

Salt and freshly ground black pepper, to taste

Cayenne to taste

1 teaspoon ground allspice

1 teaspoon ground nutmeg

1 tablespoon ground cumin

2 tablespoons of olive oil

INSTRUCTIONS

1. Sauté the onions and celery until translucent.
2. Add the garlic and the pumpkin. Continue to sauté for 5 minutes.
3. Cover with the chicken stock. Bring to a boil, then reduce to a simmer.
4. Season with salt, pepper, allspice, nutmeg, cumin, and cayenne. Cook until pumpkin is soft, about 25 to 30 minutes.
5. Puree the pumpkin with an immersion blender or a regular blender (or food processor). Please note: make sure that your blender or food processor can be used with hot liquids. Some blenders require that the soup must be totally cooled before blending.
6. Return the soup to the pot and add the lamb meatballs and kale and simmer on medium to medium-low until the meatballs are fully cooked and the kale is softened, about 25 minutes.

Roasted Eggplant and Tomato Soup

I mentioned earlier that I have only recently become a fan of eggplant (or aubergine, as they say in the Holy Land), but I have always loved tomatoes. At one point in my life—very early on, I might add—tomatoes were the only vegetable I would eat. Besides corn. And don't start on the whole tomato-is-a-fruit-not-a-vegetable-thing. Try explaining that to a seven year old. They all know it's really a vegetable.

When you think of soup, you might be tempted to think that you just throw everything in the pot and pour some water on top, turn the heat up, and you're done. You *could* do that, of course. But I wouldn't recommend it.

This soup does call for chicken stock. four cups, in fact. But this soup is also pureed. If you prefer a soup that is chunkier, you can refrain from pureeing it. But you might also want to add a little more stock. Experiment. Taste and see. Make it according to your taste.

The only thing you can't change is the roasting part. Yes, you must roast the veggies first for this soup. It might seem like an extra step, but it is oh-so-worth-it. Roasting the eggplant, tomatoes, onions, and garlic before adding them to the stock intensifies and deepens their flavors. It's really what makes this soup.

If you're not big on creamy soups, just reduce the amount of cream called for, or toss it out completely. This soup will be good either way.

INGREDIENTS

2 medium eggplants, halved lengthwise

3 ripe tomatoes, halved

2 medium sweet yellow onions, peeled and halved

6 to 8 cloves of garlic

Extra virgin olive oil (to drizzle over vegetables for roasting)

1 teaspoon dried thyme

2 teaspoons cumin

½ to 1 teaspoon cayenne or crushed red pepper flakes (optional)

4 cups chicken stock

¼ cup heavy whipping cream

¾ cup Feta cheese, crumbled

Kosher salt and freshly cracked black pepper, to taste

Lemon wedges, as garnish

INSTRUCTIONS

1. Preheat oven to 400 degrees.
2. Place eggplant, tomatoes, onion, and garlic on a large baking sheet (or two smaller baking sheets if they won't fit on just one), and drizzle with olive oil. Roast in the oven for about 45 minutes, checking on the garlic after 30 minutes to make sure it doesn't burn. Pull the garlic whenever it is ready, peel it, then set it aside. The goal here is to roast the vegetables until they are tender and start to brown.
3. Remove the vegetables from the oven and allow to cool just enough so that you can handle the eggplant. Using a large spoon, scoop out the flesh of the eggplant and place in a large heavy-bottomed soup pot. Discard the eggplant skins.
4. Add the tomatoes, onions, and garlic to the pot with the eggplant. Add the thyme and the chicken stock and bring to a boil. Immediately reduce heat to a simmer and cook for about 45 minutes. You are looking for the onions to become very tender.
5. Using an immersion blender, puree the soup. If you don't have an immersion blender, you can do the same thing by transferring the soup in batches to a food processor or blender (just make sure your

blender can handle hot soup!). Puree and return to the pot.

6. Add the cream and bring the soup back to a simmer. Taste and season with salt and pepper, and adjust any of the other seasonings.

7. Serve hot in bowls. Top with crumbled Feta. You can also squeeze some fresh lemon juice over the soup in each bowl.

Carrot Soup with Roasted Chickpeas

I don't eat carrots raw. They're OK shredded and tossed in a salad, but I had a bad experience with raw carrots when I ran track in high school. Cooked carrots are a different matter entirely. As a matter of fact, anytime I think of cooked carrots, my brain naturally gravitates to a side dish served in Picadilly Cafeterias: Carrot Souffle. I'm telling you, I often wonder if they don't put something in that dish that makes people crave it. Besides sugar, I mean. I use carrots in soups all the time. I also reserve the washed skins and tops of carrots for my stocks, and even add extra chunks of carrots. Carrots are sweet by nature and they bring that sweetness to whatever they are added to. This soup is made with two pounds of sautéed carrots, but the sweetness is not overpowering. The garlic and Middle Eastern seasonings balance it out. The white wine vinegar helps too.

Just like the Roasted Eggplant Soup, if you prefer a chunkier soup refrain from using the immersion blender. You just might want to add a little extra stock to the soup.

I love the nuttiness of the Tahini Sauce, but Labneh can be used instead. Labneh would make the soup a bit creamier.

Finally, the roasted chickpeas are, well, simply amazing. They add a spicy-crunchiness that makes this soup pop. If you don't have chickpeas on hand, you can serve the soup with toasted Arabic Bread.

INGREDIENTS

For the Soup:

2 pounds carrots, peeled and sliced thinly

2 medium sweet yellow onions, chopped

6 garlic cloves, crushed

1 teaspoon ground cumin

1 teaspoon allspice

½ teaspoon ground coriander

Kosher salt, to taste

Pinch of red pepper flakes

4 cups chicken stock

2 tablespoons extra virgin olive oil

White wine vinegar, to taste

For the Garnish:

Creamy Tahini Sauce (recipe page 44)

½ bunch fresh parsley, chopped

Za'atar or toasted sesame seeds

2 cups of roasted chickpeas (see next page)

INSTRUCTIONS

1. In a large soup pot, heat the olive oil over medium heat.
2. Add the carrots, onions, garlic, coriander, cumin, allspice, 1 teaspoon of the salt, and the red pepper flakes. Sauté until they begin to brown, about 15 minutes, stirring occasionally to prevent burning.
3. Add the chicken stock, making sure that you scrape the bottom of the pot to deglaze any browned bits and pieces. Bring the soup to a boil, then immediately reduce the heat to maintain a simmer. Simmer until the carrots are tender, about 30 minutes.
4. Using an immersion blender, puree the soup. If you don't have an immersion blender, you can do the same thing by transferring the soup in batches to a food processor or blender (just make sure that your blender can handle hot soup!). Puree and return to the pot and allow to simmer.
5. Season the soup to taste with olive oil, salt, and white wine vinegar.
6. Serve the soup in bowls, and garnish each bowl with a dollop of the Creamy Tahini Sauce, a pinch of Za'atar, or toasted sesame seeds, 10 to 12 roasted chickpeas, and the chopped parsley.

To Roast the Chickpeas:

Roasting the chickpeas is a simple process and can be done ahead of time.

1. Preheat the oven to 400.

2. In a mixing bowl, combine 1-15 oz. can of chickpeas, drained and rinsed (or the equivalent in prepared dried chickpeas), 1 tablespoon of olive oil, 1 teaspoon each of kosher salt and cumin and sumac, and ½ teaspoon of cayenne. You can even add a dash of Za'atar.

3. Mix together well and transfer to a baking sheet. Spread the chickpeas out into a single layer and roast in the oven for about 30 minutes. You are looking for them to turn golden brown.

4. The end result will be a crunchy and tasty little chickpea that perfectly accompanies this carrot soup.

Tomato Soup with Rice and Lamb

Lamb shanks are the key. You can start this soup from water, if you want, because the bone-in shanks will give you the flavor you need.

This is one of the few soups I make that has no onion and no garlic. But the shanks are on center stage, and I don't want anything to take away from that. The seasoning is there to help bring out the natural flavor of the shanks. The tomatoes are there just to serve as a base.

There is no measurement for the liquid. Play with it. See what you like. Since you have 1 cup of rice, you know that you'll need at least 2 cups of water. But you'll need more than that to cover the shanks. Do what tastes right....And enjoy.

INGREDIENTS

2 lamb shanks (can substitute beef)

Water or stock (chicken or beef), just enough to cover the shanks

1 cup long grain rice

1 pound of ripe tomatoes, crushed (can substitute 1-28 oz. can of whole plum tomatoes, crushed)

1 teaspoon cinnamon

1 teaspoon allspice

½ teaspoon cayenne (optional)

Kosher salt and freshly cracked black pepper, to taste

INSTRUCTIONS

1. Place the shanks in a large heavy-bottomed pot. Add enough water to just cover the shanks. Bring to a boil, then immediately reduce heat to medium or medium-low to maintain a simmer. Cover and simmer until tender, about 1 hour. Skim and discard any fat that accumulates.

2. Stir in the rice and the spices and cook for 20 minutes. Add the tomatoes, season with salt and pepper, and simmer for about 20 minutes.

Lamb and Vegetable Soup

This soup is similar to the Lamb and Tomato Stew with Crispy Potatoes I shared with you on (page 88) However, this is a soup, not a stew, so it is not as thick. It also has its own flavor profile. This soup is more in line with what I cook on a regular basis. Life is busy and I do have a family of five to feed. There are fewer steps to this soup, compared to the stew. I can put this one on the stove and let it simmer while I take care of other pressing matters.

The celery here is something different for us. My wife and I are not huge fans of celery, which is difficult for anybody who grew up in south Louisiana. Down here we have our very own culinary "trinity" which is used in many Cajun and Creole dishes. They are so prevalent—and Catholicism is so much a part and parcel of our daily experience in south Louisiana—that these three vegetables have been dubbed "*the holy trinity.*" I'm talking about onions, celery, and bell pepper. I keep trying to tell anybody who will listen that we should swap out the celery for garlic, but nobody is listening.

It doesn't matter. Celery is not evil and this soup is really delicious.

INGREDIENTS

2 to 3 lamb shanks (can substitute beef)

12 cups beef stock, to start. You might need increase this depending on how dense you want your soup (can substitute chicken stock or water)

2 medium sweet yellow onions, chopped

1 stalk of celery, finely chopped

3 carrots, cubed

2 pounds of potatoes, cubed

1 pound fresh string beans, cut into bite-sized pieces

3 ripe tomatoes, diced (can substitute 1-28 oz. can of petite diced tomatoes)

½ bunch of parsley, finely chopped

1 teaspoon cinnamon

1 teaspoon cumin

1 teaspoon allspice

½ to 1 teaspoon cayenne (optional)

Kosher salt and freshly cracked black pepper, to taste

INSTRUCTIONS

1. Place the shanks in a large heavy-bottomed pot. Add the stock and bring to a boil. Immediately reduce heat to medium or medium-low to maintain a simmer. Cover and simmer until tender, about 1 hour. Skim and discard any fat that accumulates.
2. Prep all the vegetables, cubing the potatoes and carrots at about the same size (bite-sized) for even cooking.
3. Add the onions, celery, carrots, potatoes, and string beans to the pot along with the tomatoes and the seasonings. Cook until the vegetables are tender, about 20 minutes.
4. Taste and adjust seasoning as necessary. Add the chopped parsley the last 5 minutes of cooking.
5. Serve hot in bowls and garnish with a dash of cinnamon.

Jerusalem Artichoke Soup

I've always been fascinated with Jerusalem artichokes. The name has always intrigued me. Artichokes are another thing my wife challenged me to taste. Of course, she had a distinct advantage since the artichoke she was trying to get me to taste was a Seafood-Stuffed Artichoke that her mom had made. I was already tempted to taste it because of all the shrimp and lump crabmeat. I was completely willing to ignore the fact that the seafood was in an artichoke! Needless to say, I liked it. So now I eat artichokes. Yum!

Jerusalem artichokes are different though. They are not really artichokes at all. They are part of the sunflower family. But the roots taste like artichokes, and they have been very popular in culinary circles for the last few years.

This recipe combines two starches: Jerusalem artichokes and potatoes. This is a cream-based soup, and it is pureed. As mentioned before, you can opt to not puree the soup. Also, feel free to reduce or eliminate the cream, though I really like cream in my root vegetable soups, whether Jerusalem artichokes or potato. This recipe was inspired by a recipe that Chef Nabil Aho gave me on my first trip to the Holy Land.

INGREDIENTS

1 ½ pounds Jerusalem artichokes, peeled and cut 1/2-inch slices

1 large sweet yellow onion, finely chopped

2 clove of garlic, crushed

2 tablespoons of unsalted butter

8½ cups fresh chicken stock (see page 80)

1 cup potatoes, peeled and sliced

1 cup heavy whipping cream

Kosher salt and freshly cracked black pepper, to taste

Parsley, finely chopped for garnish

INSTRUCTIONS

1. In a soup pot over medium-high heat, sauté the onion in the butter until the onion starts to become translucent. Add the garlic and sauté for another minute or two, stirring constantly to avoid burning the garlic. Add the Jerusalem artichokes, the potatoes, and the chicken stock to the pot and season with the salt and black pepper.

2. Allow the soup to come to a boil, then immediately reduce heat to maintain a simmer. Simmer until the artichokes and potatoes are tender, about 30 to 35 minutes.

3. Add the cream and puree the soup either with an immersion blender, or in batches in a blender or food processor.

4. Taste. Adjust seasoning, as necessary. Serve in bowls and garnish with chopped parsley.

NOTE: COMPLEX SOUP

For a more complex flavor profile on this soup, roast about half of the Jerusalem artichokes first. Peel them, but keep them whole. Drizzle with olive oil and sprinkle a little salt and black pepper on them. Roast them in a preheated oven (450 degrees) for 30 to 45 minutes, until tender. When you add the sliced Jerusalem artichokes and the potatoes to the pot, you can quarter the roasted artichokes and add them to the pot at the same time.

Creamy Tomato Soup

Soup is good food, or so says the old Campbell's Soup commercials from the 1970s. I think it was the 70s. Maybe it was the 80s. Either way, I still hear that jingle in my head when I talk about soup.

Whether in a pizza sauce, a pasta sauce, a soup, or by themselves, sliced on a plate and sprinkled with salt and pepper, I have always loved tomatoes. Here in south Louisiana we have a special tomato that we call "Creole." I grew up thinking Creole tomatoes were a different variety of tomato because their taste was so distinct, a little extra tang and bite. It was only much later in life that I learned they are not a different variety. They are simply homegrown tomatoes. What gives them their unique taste is the soil they are grown in. There is something in the soil in southeast Louisiana that makes the tomatoes "Creole."

It's the same thing with Vidalia onions. They're just sweet yellow onions, but they are grown in Vidalia, Georgia. There is something about the soil in Vidalia that makes those onions sweeter than other sweet yellow onions.

I confess that I have a hard time putting fresh Creole tomatoes in soup. In Shrimp or Crawfish Étouffée, yes. In a gumbo, yes. I have no problem with that. But tomatoes can get lost in a soup. They have a tendency to cook down to nothing. For the recipe below, I call for either canned tomatoes or the Pomi brand, which comes in a box. You can certainly use fresh tomatoes if you prefer. But using canned or boxed tomatoes will allow you to make this soup any time of the year.

INGREDIENTS

2 boxes (26 oz. each) of Pomi chopped tomatoes (or 2-28 oz. cans of chopped tomatoes)

2 cups chicken stock

1 large onion, chopped

2 medium carrots, grated

3 to 4 cloves of garlic, minced

3 tablespoons extra virgin olive oil

2 tablespoons butter

1 teaspoon ground allspice

1 teaspoon ground cumin

2 Bay leaves

½ cup to 1 cup of Half and Half (or ½ cup of heavy cream)

Coarse ground kosher salt & freshly ground black pepper, to taste

Crushed red pepper flakes, to taste

INSTRUCTIONS

1. Heat olive oil in a soup pot over medium heat.
2. Add the onion and carrots and sauté until softened (about 10 minutes). Add the garlic during the last minute or two, stirring constantly to prevent burning.
3. Add the tomatoes, the chicken stock, Bay leaves, butter and seasoning.
4. Simmer until the veggies are tender, about 30 minutes.
5. Remove the Bay leaves and add the cream or Half and Half.
6. Puree with a hand held immersion blender until smooth.

Sides

Steamed Vegetables

Carrots with Cumin

Salty-sweet. I love that taste. My favorite chocolate bar is dark chocolate with sea salt. My favorite ice cream flavor is salted caramel. See the pattern?

This carrot dish follows suit. Carrots are naturally sweet, and roasting them intensifies their flavor. Toss in a little salt, cumin, and red pepper flakes, and you have an easy-to-make savory side dish that pairs well with just about any Middle Eastern meat or fish dish.

If you can get your hands on fresh baby carrots, that would be preferable. If not, you can use full-sized carrots, but you will have to cut them into sticks. Just make sure you maintain consistency in the size of the sticks for even cooking.

INGREDIENTS

1 to 1½ pounds of baby carrots, trimmed (or full carrots cut into sticks)

3 tablespoons of extra virgin olive oil

2 teaspoons of ground cumin

½ teaspoon of ground coriander

¼ teaspoon crushed red pepper flakes, or to taste (optional)

Kosher salt and freshly ground black pepper, to taste

Sprigs of fresh cilantro, as garnish

INSTRUCTIONS

1. Preheat the oven to 425 degrees.
2. In a mixing bowl, combine the olive oil and the seasonings. Mix together well.
3. Add the carrots to the mixing bowl and toss with the olive oil mixture. (Using your hands for this task is not only more effective at evenly coating the carrots, it is also fun.)
4. Place the carrots in a single layer on a large baking dish and roast until soft and turning brown, about 25 to 30 minutes. Serve hot, garnished with sprigs of fresh cilantro.

Sautéed Dandelion Greens with Caramelized Onions

On my recent Food Meets Faith pilgrimage to the Holy Land, I had the pleasure of spending a day in Jericho, which is believed to be the oldest continually inhabited city in the world. It was a Sunday, and after touring around the old section of Jericho, we stopped at Good Shepherd Church for Mass.

Lunch arrangements had been planned ahead of time, and it included a tour of a local farm that provides the greens for The Green Valley, the restaurant we were to eat at. The restaurant—and the garden—was owned by local Christian families.

Even though it was February, the weather had already started to warm up in The Holy Land, and the first signs of spring were budding forth. There were all kinds of greens there. Our guides knew the names of the various greens in Arabic and Hebrew, but not in English. We walked through the garden tasting the different greens to try to determine what the English names were….a task that was a bit more difficult than I imagined it would be, mainly because not all of the greens looked the same as their American counterparts. Take the arugula for example. In Arabic it is called *Jar Jeer*, but it looked very different from the arugula I am used to seeing.

The green leaves of spring in Palestine are abundant in February, March, and April. They grow everywhere: in the cracks of sidewalks, on the side of the road, in small gardens, and, of course, up in the mountains. Some people might think that the greens look like grass, or even weeds, but Palestinians have used them as an integral part of their diet for as long as anybody can remember.

The most well known greens are *Hindbeh* (dandelion), *Hwerneh* (hedge mustard greens), *Jar Jeer* (arugula), *Khubbeizeh* (wild mallows), Swiss Chard, and *Baqleh* (purslane). They are plentiful in the area of Jericho, and for the most part, they are free for the picking.

Dandelion greens pack a punch when it comes to nutrition. They could very well be called a "super green." And they are not short on taste either. They are a bit bitter when eaten raw, but a little olive oil, lemon juice, and garlic will go a long way in mellowing out the bitterness.

Since I love sautéed mustard greens and collard greens, I thought that dandelion greens would go well with caramelized onions and garlic, lemon, and olive oil. Boy, was I right! Dandelion greens are often available at farmers markets across the United States in the spring. Get your hands on some and try out this delicious—and nutritious!—recipe!

INGREDIENTS

8 packed cups of chopped dandelion greens

½ cup extra-virgin olive oil, plus a little extra for drizzling

2 cups sweet yellow onions, thinly sliced

Juice of 1 lemon

1 teaspoon kosher salt, or to taste

½ teaspoon freshly ground black pepper, or to taste

A dash or two of cayenne, *optional*

Lemon wedges as garnish

INSTRUCTIONS

To Prepare the Dandelion Greens
1. Thoroughly wash the greens, making sure to rinse out any deeply embedded dirt and debris, then shake out the excess water and set aside.
2. Cut the greens into 2-inch strips (width-wise), and steam them to soften, just until they begin to wilt. (Alternatively, you can blanch the greens in boiling water for a minute or two, until they soften.)
3. Set aside in a strainer so that excess water can drain out. Once the greens are cool enough to handle, you can use your hands to squeeze out any remaining water.

Caramelize the Onions and Add the Dandelion Greens
1. Preheat a heavy-bottomed stainless steel skillet over medium-high heat.
2. Add ½ cup of olive oil, the onions, and a pinch or two of salt. Stir well to coat the onions in the olive oil, and sauté until golden brown.
3. Using a slotted spoon, remove enough of the onions to top each finished serving and set aside.
4. Add the dandelion greens to the skillet and season with salt and pepper. Sauté, stirring occasionally, for 7 to 10 minutes.
5. During the last minute or two of cooking, add the lemon juice and stir well to incorporate.
6. The greens can be transferred to a serving dish. Top with the caramelized onions and garnish with the lemon wedges.

Arabic Rice with Lamb

I grew up eating Jambalaya, which is a spicy Louisiana dish of rice, chicken, and pork sausage. I still remember the day when I discovered meat came from animals and didn't just magically appear in plastic wrap at the local grocery store. I looked at my mom and asked, "So I'm eating rice, chicken, and pigs?" I never looked at my food the same again. I had another culinary learning experience when I was a seminarian in formation with Mother Teresa's priests, the Missionaries of Charity Fathers, in Tijuana, Mexico. That was back in 1989 to 1991. I was 18 when I arrived in Mexico, and I spoke no Spanish. I might have been in Mexico for only a week or two when I learned what it really meant to "run around like a chicken with its head cut off."

That was something that really impressed me about the Holy Land. Food was fresh, and you always knew where it came from. Everything was fresh and local. Food doesn't have to travel far. Geographically, The Holy Land is just a little smaller than the state of New Jersey, which means it doesn't take long to get produce from farm to table.

The two main ingredients of this dish, lamb, and rice, are both staples. They are both plentiful and are used in numerous recipes. Put them together in this recipe, though, and you will have a side dish you wished was a main course. It's that good.

When cooking rice for a dish like this (as with the Rice Pilaf), most cookbooks will tell you to "reduce the heat to low and simmer for…" But I have found that there is a big difference in temperature control among stoves. My stove set on low might be hotter than your stove set on the same dial reading. The important thing is not what the dial says, rather it is that the rice continues to simmer at the lowest possible temperature. For my stove, that's somewhere between low and medium-low. It may very well be different for your stove.

INGREDIENTS

1½ pounds ground lamb

2 cups long-grain rice (Jasmine or Basmati)

3 tablespoons of butter

3½ cups chicken stock, boiling (note: In recipes that call for chicken stock, I use homemade stock that contains no salt. Be mindful that most store-bought stocks contain salt, which means that you will need to adjust the amount of salt called for in this recipe).

2 teaspoons salt, or to taste

½ teaspoon freshly ground black pepper

1 teaspoon allspice

1 teaspoon nutmeg

1 teaspoon cinnamon

½ cup pine nuts, toasted

Parsley, chopped, as garnish

INSTRUCTIONS

1. In a large deep skillet, over medium-high heat, lightly brown the lamb in the butter.
2. Once browned, add the rice, salt, black pepper, allspice, nutmeg, and cinnamon and stir well. Allow mixture to heat thoroughly for a minute or two.
3. Slowly add the boiling broth, stirring to incorporate. Bring to a boil, then cover and reduce heat and simmer until the rice is cooked, about 20 minutes.
4. When the rice is cooked and all the water is absorbed, remove from heat and allow to sit for 10 minutes while you toast the pine nuts.
5. To toast the pine nuts, see the box on the next page.
6. When you are ready to serve the rice, transfer to a serving dish and garnish with the pine nuts and the chopped parsley.

NOTE: TOASTING PINE NUTS

Another ingredient is pine nuts. Toasting pine nuts is a delicate task. To toast them, heat a skillet over medium heat for a couple minutes, then add the pine nuts. Toast the pine nuts in the skillet for 30 to 45 seconds, then toss them in the pan. Toast them for another 30 to 45 seconds, then toss them again. Continue this process until you see them start to turn golden. Remove them from the skillet and let them cool. You have to be careful with pine nuts. They are very easy to burn. Although you can toast them dry, I frequently add butter to the skillet for added flavor, depending on what they will be used for.

Rice Pilaf

Rice-a-Roni may be "the San Francisco treat," but this homemade Middle Eastern rice pilaf is the original, and it is so much better than the boxed version. It's amazing how much flavor this dish has. Sautéing the vermicelli in butter adds a nutty flavor to the rice, and using chicken stock to cook the rice gives this dish a depth of flavor and richness you can't get with water.

This recipe calls for salt and cinnamon as seasoning and parsley for garnish, but you can get creative with this dish. Add cayenne, or coriander, or cumin. Try cilantro instead of parsley. Add lemon. Top with a dollop of Labneh. There are so many things you can do with this basic recipe. Some of our favorite dishes are born out of a little experimentation in the kitchen. I like to call it *play*. I play in the kitchen, and it's always fun!

INGREDIENTS

1 cup of vermicelli, broken into ½ inch pieces

3 tablespoons butter or olive oil

2 cups jasmine long-grain rice

4 cups chicken stock, boiling

1½ teaspoons salt, or to taste (the amount of salt you add will depend on whether you use salted or unsalted stock)

1 pinch of ground cinnamon, as garnish

Parsley, chopped, as garnish

INSTRUCTIONS

1. Sauté vermicelli, stirring constantly over medium-high heat until brown. Be careful not to burn it.
2. Add rice and salt and stir well.
3. Slowly add the boiling broth, stirring to incorporate. Bring back to a boil, cover and reduce heat to low. Allow to simmer until the rice is cooked, about 20 minutes.
4. Uncover and gently fluff the rice with a fork. Transfer to a serving dish and garnish with chopped parsley and a pinch (or more!) of ground cinnamon.

Turkish Salad

This dish is called a salad, but it's more like a dip or a side dish, and it is often found on the table as a Mezze. This Turkish Salad was a hit with our group. There were four or five plates of this on our table at Abu Shanab where we had lunch one day in Bethlehem, and we wiped all those plates clean!

This is a "cooked" salad, but traditionally it is served chilled. It can be served as a side dish or as part of a Mezze. Serve it with hot Pita bread. It can also be used as a dip for carrot sticks, celery sticks, or sliced cucumbers.

INGREDIENTS

2 medium sweet yellow onions, diced

4 medium sweet red and green bell peppers, diced

1 to 2 jalapeño peppers, seeded and diced (depending on how hot you want this dish)

2 cloves of garlic, crushed

3 cups of canned crushed tomatoes

2 tablespoons of extra virgin olive oil

2 tablespoons of white wine vinegar

1 teaspoons of salt, or to taste

½ teaspoon freshly ground black pepper

1 teaspoon of cumin, or to taste

Parsley, chopped

INSTRUCTIONS

1. In a large skillet, sauté the onions in the olive oil over medium heat until they start to soften. Add the garlic and sauté for another minute or two, stirring to prevent burning the garlic.
2. Add the peppers, the tomatoes, the salt, pepper and cumin, and the white wine vinegar. Stir well to incorporate.
3. Bring to a boil, then reduce heat and simmer for 30 minutes.
4. Remove from heat, transfer to a serving dish and refrigerate for an hour before serving.

Steamed Mixed Vegetables

Steaming vegetables is easy to do, and it's good for you too! I was so impressed with the simplicity and the flavor of the steamed fennel root, radishes, potatoes, and garlic which accompanied my Saint Peter's Fish at Magdalena Restaurant in Tiberias.

You can steam any kind of vegetable, and doing so helps to retain the vegetable's color, texture, natural flavor, as well as its nutritional content. Steaming is a simple process that can be done in minutes.

Some common vegetables to steam: asparagus, broccoli, brussels sprouts, carrots, cauliflower, fennel, garlic, green beans, mushrooms, and zucchini.

To steam vegetables, you will need:
- a large pot and
- a steamer basket or colander that fits inside the pot.

INSTRUCTIONS
1. Fill the pot with water to just below the bottom of the basket or colander, and bring it to a boil.
2. Place the vegetables in the basket or colander and cover the pot with a loose-fitting lid so the steam can escape. Cook time varies depending on the size and thickness of the vegetables, but generally the cook time will be under 10 minutes.

If you want to boost the flavor of your steamed vegetables, here are a few things you can do:
- Sprinkle fresh herbs over the vegetables while they are steaming.
- Add slices of garlic.
- Add lemon slices.
- Use stock instead of water.
- Add soy sauce or red wine vinegar to the water (or crab boil if you like things hot and spicy!).
- Add salt or cayenne to the water.

Roasted Cauliflower (and Other Vegetables)

Like eggplant, I seemed to see cauliflower everywhere in the Holy Land. And, like eggplant, cauliflower wasn't "my favorite kind of chicken." But that's different now. I've converted. I had plenty of opportunities to eat cauliflower in The Holy Land. I had it as a topping on a Falafel sandwich, as something to dip in my Hummus instead of Pita, as part of a Makloubeh (the famous upside-down dish of the Middle East), and even all by itself roasted with a squeeze of lemon and a dash of salt.

Roasting vegetables is easy to do and it yields amazing results. Add a little olive oil, salt, and pepper, and let the dry heat of the oven work its magic. Roasting makes vegetables perfectly tender on the inside while caramelizing the outside. The result is an intensification of the natural flavor of the vegetable.

The trick to helping the caramelization process when roasting is flat surfaces. You want to cut your vegetables in such a way that they lay flat in the roasting pan. With cauliflower, for example, this can be done by slicing each floret into 1/2-inch or so thick pieces. If you cut them too thin, they will be unable to hold their shape.

This same basic recipe can be used to roast just about any vegetable, like squash, zucchini, eggplant, potatoes, carrots, peppers, broccoli, onions, tomatoes, asparagus… anything!

You can also play around with the seasoning. Instead of thyme, use oregano….or curry powder, or cumin!

INGREDIENTS

1 head of cauliflower, cut into florets

¼ cup extra virgin olive oil

5 cloves of garlic, roughly chopped

¼ teaspoon crushed red pepper flakes

2 teaspoons kosher salt

1 teaspoon dried thyme

INSTRUCTIONS

1. Preheat the oven to 450 degrees.
2. In a mixing bowl, toss together the cauliflower with olive oil, salt, red pepper flakes, garlic, and thyme. Mix together well.
3. Transfer to a large baking sheet on a single layer. Roast in the oven for about 20 minutes, until golden and tender.

Smothered Green Beans

Growing up in south Louisiana means that I am no stranger to anything smothered. Crawfish Étouffée, or Shrimp or Chicken Étouffée, are all smothered dishes. As a matter of fact, the word *étouffée* means *smothered*. Grillades & Grits (pronounced "greeyahds" with the accent on the "gree.") is another smothered dish. *Smothered* in south Louisiana typically means smothered in onions, bell peppers, and celery. Otherwise known as the "holy trinity" of Cajun and Creole cooking.

In the Holy Land, I was happy to discover we weren't the only ones to smother our veggies. The addition of the olive oil and the sweet yellow onion gives a sweetness to the green beans, while the lemon gives them a little tang. I bet these green beans would be mouthwatering roasted too.

INGREDIENTS

1 pound fresh green beans

1 large sweet yellow onion, chopped

1 teaspoon kosher salt, or to taste

½ teaspoon freshly cracked black pepper

¼ cup extra virgin olive oil

Lemon wedges, as garnish

INSTRUCTIONS

1. Rinse and drain the green beans, set aside.
2. In a skillet over medium-high heat, sauté the onions in olive oil until golden brown, about 12 to 15 minutes.
3. Add the green beans and season with salt and pepper.
4. Cover, reduce heat to low or medium-low and cook for about 30 minutes, stirring occasionally.
5. Serve as a side. Squeeze a little fresh lemon juice on top.

Middle Eastern Mashed Potatoes

Mashed potatoes are just plain good. But these mashed potatoes will be like nothing you have ever tasted. The addition of lemon juice and mint is very un-American, but oh-so-good!

Even though I used extra virgin olive oil instead of butter, I can't help but feel like adding a little butter on top of the potatoes when I plate them. I'm a creature of habit, I guess.

Potatoes absorb water when they are boiled, so I always make sure to salt my water first. Doing so will insure that the potatoes are salted throughout. Once they are fully cooked, and I add the rest of the ingredients, I always taste to see if I need to add more salt. There is nothing worse than over-salted food, so I add it slowly. Remember, it's easy to add salt, but impossible to take it out. Add it slowly, and taste frequently.

For a twist on this recipe, add a little full-fat Greek yogurt or Labneh. The yogurt intensifies the tang of the lemon and it makes the potatoes creamier. But it's optional.

INGREDIENTS

4 large potatoes, cut in chunks

1 medium sweet yellow onion, finely chopped

½ cup extra virgin olive oil

1 tablespoon of fresh mint, finely chopped

Juice of 1 lemon

Kosher salt and freshly cracked black pepper, to taste

INSTRUCTIONS

1. In a large pot, cover the potatoes with water. Salt the water to taste and bring to a boil. Cook until soft.
2. Drain the potatoes, return to the pot, and mash.
3. Add the onion, olive oil, pepper, and lemon juice, and mix together well until the potatoes are fluffy. Taste and adjust salt.
4. Serve as a side and top with fresh mint.

Mujadra or Mujadara

In our extended family we call this dish Mujadra, or even Jadra for short. But, like many Middle Eastern dishes, this one can have different spellings and pronunciations. It's also known as Mujadara, or Moujadara, or Mejadra. In the region of the Middle East there are several different cultures and languages. They all eat the same foods, but the names of the food may vary from place to place. Add to this scenario the fact that immigrants to the United States a couple of generations ago wanted to simultaneously blend in and retain their cultural identity and heritage, then it becomes easier to understand why it can be so difficult to come to a consensus on how certain foods are named, spelled, and prepared.

No matter how you spell it, though, Mujadra is a dish of lentils and rice topped with caramelized onions. And what could be more basic than beans and rice?

This is the dish that introduced me to lentils. My wife and kids used to eat it at least once a week, but I never tried it. I had tasted lentils years ago and thought I did not like them. But my wife, loving me the way she does, couldn't let me miss out on something so appetizing. So she challenged me. Again. That's when I discovered I love lentils. (Thank you, Honey!)

Since I have started eating Mujadra, I have been amazed at the flavor (and nutrition) lentils pack. The olive oil and the caramelized onions add a sweetness and a depth to what would otherwise be just beans and rice. This one is a family favorite. Not only is this a dish we make at least weekly, it's also one we like to serve as a main course on Fridays in Lent.

Mujadra is tasty, quick, and easy to make. It can be served as the main course (especially in Lent!) or as a side dish. It's delicious either way! Mujadra is a great one-pot meal that can be served at table from a serving dish. Mujadra actually thickens as it cools so it can be served hot or at room temperature.

INGREDIENTS

2 cups dried lentils

8 cups of water

1 cup uncooked white rice (we use jasmine or basmati)

2 large onions, chopped

4 tablespoons of extra-virgin olive oil

1 teaspoon of freshly cracked black pepper (or to taste)

1 teaspoon cumin (or to taste)

Kosher salt to taste

Fresh chopped parsley as a garnish

INSTRUCTIONS

1. Rinse lentils and add to a pot with cold water (all 8 cups).
2. Bring to a boil, and boil on medium-high heat for 20 minutes.
3. In the meantime, sauté the onions in the olive oil on medium-high heat.
4. When the onions start to brown nicely, add the onions and olive oil (along with any brown caramelized bits) to the pot. Also add the rice, salt, pepper, and cumin.
5. Stir to mix well, then cover and cook for 20 minutes. Stir occasionally to prevent scorching.

Parsley Potatoes

I mentioned earlier, I used to think parsley was just for decoration. It's what restaurants would put on the side of your plate to give it a little extra color. Growing up, I don't think I ever saw anyone eat parsley. Who wants to eat a decoration?

But parsley is used extensively in Middle Eastern cuisine. Tabbouleh is a parsley salad. There is another parsley salad, topped with a tahini dressing, that is popular in Palestine, and there are many dishes that include parsley.

Parsley does indeed have a taste, and it's a good one that beautifully enhances these boiled red potatoes. I prefer to use small, or baby, red potatoes, but you can use larger ones and just cut them into smaller chunks. Add a bit of garlic and butter, salt and black pepper, and you have an easy-to-prepare side dish that will pair nicely next to any meat or fish.

INGREDIENTS

12 to 15 small red potatoes, cleaned and cut in half

1 clove of garlic, crushed

½ stick of butter

Kosher salt and freshly cracked black pepper to taste

⅓ cup of fresh parsley, finely chopped

INSTRUCTIONS

1. Add the potatoes to a medium-sized heavy-bottomed pot and cover with cold water.
2. Bring to a boil over high heat and cook until a fork can easily pierce the potatoes, about 10 to 15 minutes.
3. Remove from heat and drain.
4. Return the potatoes to the pot over medium heat and add the butter and parsley. Stir to combine well.
5. Cover and cook for about 10 minutes, stirring occasionally.
6. Add salt and black pepper to taste.

Crispy Roasted Potatoes

I was genuinely surprised by all the French fries I saw in the Holy Land. I guess I always assumed that French fries were so American. But we were served French fries at a few very nice restaurants.

Frying is one of those cooking methods that has always given me trouble. Pan-frying is easy, but *frying*....not so much. I think the biggest difficulty is temperature control. I find it difficult to maintain the right temperature. If the oil is too hot, you can either burn the food, or the outside cooks but the inside is still raw. I did that frying chicken before. If your oil is not hot enough, your foods will come out saturated with oil....and undercooked.

Did I mention that frying inside stinks up the house? For all of these reasons, I rarely fry anything, and when I think about frying, the voice of Chef Emeril Lagasse rings in my ears, "Fry right or don't fry at all."

So, what do you do when you want to have potatoes that are crispy on the outside and soft as butter on the inside but you can't fry?

You combine the methods of parboiling and roasting to mimic the crispiness of frying. This is a technique I learned a while back from *Cooks Illustrated*. Parboiling the potatoes draws out starch and sugar to the surface of the potato slices. When you roughen those surfaces by tossing the parboiled potatoes with olive oil and salt, you create a surface that crisps up really well when the potatoes are roasted. This method takes longer, that's true. But the results are worth it. You end up with "healthy French fries."

INGREDIENTS

3 pounds Yellow Yukon Gold potatoes

4 tablespoons olive oil

3 teaspoons of salt

Freshly chopped parsley, as garnish

INSTRUCTIONS

1. Parboil the potatoes. To do so, thoroughly wash them and cut them into 1/2-inch thick rounds. Place them in a large pot and cover with cold water, making sure the potatoes are covered by at least an inch of water. Add 1 teaspoon of salt to the pot and bring to a boil over high heat. Once they come to a boil, you may need to turn the heat down a little bit, but allow them to boil for about 5 minutes. You don't want the potatoes to fully cook. You are only looking to parboil the potatoes and to draw out some of the starch and sugar from the potatoes.

2. Drain the potatoes and transfer them to a large mixing bowl. Working quickly, add 2 tablespoons of olive oil and ½ teaspoon of salt, and mix together well using a rubber spatula. After mixing well, add another 2 tablespoons of olive oil and another ½ teaspoon of salt. Once the potatoes start to look and feel pasty on the outside transfer them to a large baking sheet, laying them out in a single layer. Use two baking sheets if necessary.

3. Place on the lowest racks in the oven and bake at 450 degrees for about 20 minutes.

4. Once the potatoes are crispy on the bottom, remove the baking sheets from the oven and carefully flip the potatoes. Return baking sheets to oven and continue to bake for another 10 to 15 minutes. Remove from oven and transfer the potatoes to a cooling rack, or serve immediately.

Entrees: Chicken, Lamb, and Beef

This is how it looks in the pot...

This is how it looks on the plate...

Makloubeh, see page 154

Shish Kebabs: Beef, Lamb, or Chicken

In my family certain members are known for certain dishes, and cousin Brent Samaha is king of the Shish Kebab. (Shish Kebab refers to pieces of meat, fish, or vegetables grilled over a fire on a skewer or spit). The recipe for Shish Kebab I share with you here is an amalgamation of the recipes used by different family members. Most of the cooks in the family cook like chefs do. There are no real written recipes. Cooking is, after all, a culinary *art*.

One of my early culinary inspirations was Marcelle Bienvenu, a food writer, chef, and former restaurant owner who may be most well-known locally for a little book she published in 1991 called *Who's Your Mama, Are You Catholic, and Can You Make a Roux?* Born and raised in Saint Martinville, in southwest Louisiana, Marcelle Bienvenu grew up where she says "good cooking was almost as large an article of faith as the Catholic religion." What many people may not know about Marcelle is that she co-authored many of Chef Emeril Lagasse's early cookbooks, and she was adamant that the recipes in those books be tested in a real home kitchen, not a test kitchen.

In July of 2009, I had the pleasure of interviewing Marcelle for The Catholic Foodie podcast. I was anxious to get her professional thoughts on recipes and cooking. We had an excellent conversation about the joy of cooking, about having fun in the kitchen, about how people see recipes as "rules to follow" instead of general guidelines that give the cook lots of room to play and create. She also noted that most home cooks need recipes to start with. In the end, Marcelle's advice was to simply cook food the way you like it to taste. If you need to deviate from a recipe in order to do that, so be it. The recipe police will not come after you. Trying to get a Shish Kebab recipe from family members was no easy task. Most chefs like to guard their popular recipes and not one person in the family had a single recipe for Shish Kebab written down. I talked through the recipes with a few family members, then created a blend of their input, keeping what they all had in common, and paring down the quantities.

Shish Kebab is great for feeding a crowd. Here's one example: Tailgating at football games is a great American pastime, and my family tailgates in style. Cousin Brent Samaha makes marinade by the gallon, and usually cooks about 15 pounds of beef and 10 pounds of chicken. That might be just a bit too much for a typical family weekend meal, so I pared the quantities down to a reasonable size for a family of five, but with an eye toward "big-batch" cooking. In other words, if you are going to go through all the effort to prepare five pounds of meat for Shish Kebab, you might as well do 10 pounds and have enough to last a couple of meals. This recipe is for 10 pounds of meat: beef, chicken, or lamb.

INGREDIENTS

For the Marinade:

1 cup fresh squeeze lemon juice

½ cup extra virgin olive oil

5 teaspoons kosher salt, or to taste

2 teaspoons freshly cracked black pepper, or to taste

1½ to 2 teaspoons crushed red pepper flakes, or to taste

Handful of dried mint, crushed finely

10 cloves of garlic, minced

½ onion, finely chopped

1 to 2 jalapeño peppers, seeded and chopped

6 ounces of Worchestershire Sauce

4 ounces Louisiana Hot Sauce

For the Shish Kebab:

6 medium sweet yellow onions

5 bell peppers

Whole mushrooms (amount up to chef's discretion, but we usually do about 1 pound)

Cherry tomatoes (again, the amount is up the chef, but about 1 pound)

12 to 14 pounds of beef sirloin, or leg of lamb, or chicken

INSTRUCTIONS

Make the Marinade:

1. Add the garlic, kosher salt, black pepper, and lemon juice to a food processor and pulse until well blended.
2. Add the olive oil, crushed red pepper, Worchestershire, and mint. Pulse lightly to incorporate.
3. Cut the meat into 1 ½ to 2-inch cubes.
4. Quarter the onions and cut the bell peppers into bite-sized pieces.
5. Place the meat in a large container or in one or more resealable plastic bags. In a separate container, place the quartered onions, the bell pepper, and the whole mushrooms.
6. Divide the marinade between the containers, seal them, and refrigerate overnight.

Cooking the Shish Kebab:

1. Preheat outdoor grill to medium-high heat. Remove meat and vegetables from the refrigerator to prepare your skewers. Alternate meat and vegetables on the skewer without over-crowding it. Some people swear that there is only one way to do this, but I don't think the pattern really matters, except that it is helpful to have a piece of meat go on the skewer first so that it is at the base. Cousin Brent has a very specific pattern, and each of his skewers starts and ends with meat, and there is always onion in between each chunk of meat. The other vegetables can vary.
2. Brush each skewer with a little olive oil to prevent sticking and place them on the grill, being careful not to overcrowd the grilling surface. Cook until done, rotating at least once. Cook time will depend on how hot the grill is and how done you want the meat.

Musakhan: Palestinian Sumac Chicken

A popular dish in Palestine, enjoyed by the rich and poor alike, Musakhan can be prepared many different ways. The common denominators are chicken, onions, sumac, and bread. Sometimes you will find this dish made with bone-in chicken and served atop thick *Taboon Bread*, and other times it is made with boneless chicken rolled up in very thin Iraqi Bread rounds (or *Lafah*) and eaten like a wrap.

I have mentioned before that I love Chicken Shawarma, but that I have never made it at home. I don't have the required rig (a long metal skewer attached to a gas or electric-powered heat source) to make that work. But I have tried to make something close to a Chicken Shawarma (check out Pan-Fried Chicken with Tomato and Feta Dressing on page 146) at home.

Musakhan is similar to my Pan-Fried Chicken in that it can be eaten in a wrap like Chicken Shawarma, and the lemon juice and sumac give the chicken a tartness that reminds me of Shawarma. The only thing missing is the char that you get with the Shawarma.

I credit my friend Chef Nabil M. Aho with the inspiration behind this recipe. Chef Nabil is a member of the *Chefs for Peace* (page 18) and Head Chef Instructor of the Professional Promotion Hospitality Section of the Pontifical Institute Notre Dame of Jerusalem Center where we stayed in Jerusalem.

INGREDIENTS

2 pounds of boneless chicken thighs, chopped

¾ cup of olive oil

Juice of 2 lemons

3 large sweet yellow onion, cut into thin slivers

3 cloves of garlic, minced or crushed

½ teaspoon of ground cardamom

2 tablespoons of sumac

Coarse ground kosher salt, to taste

Freshly cracked black pepper, to taste

Cayenne, to taste

3 tablespoons pine nuts, toasted

Freshly chopped parsley, as a garnish

INSTRUCTIONS

1. Clean the chicken well and cut into large bite-sized pieces (they will shrink some as they cook). In a large mixing bowl combine the chicken with the juice of one lemon, sumac, and 2 or 3 tablespoons of olive oil. Mix together well, cover with plastic wrap, and place in refrigerator to marinate for 1 to 2 hours.

2. Add about half of the olive oil to a large skillet on medium to medium-high heat. Add onions and sauté until soft. Add the garlic, cardamom, salt, pepper, and cayenne. Continue to cook, stirring frequently, for another 5 minutes. Add the juice of the second lemon, stir, then remove contents from pan and set aside.

3. Add the remaining olive oil to the same pan, followed by the marinated chicken. Saute until golden, then add the reserved onion mixture back to the pan. Allow to cook together until the chicken is fully cooked, which should only take a few minutes. Then remove from heat.

4. To serve, spread some of the chicken and onion mixture onto thin Arabic or Iraqi Bread. Garnish with pine nuts, parsley, and Creamy Tahini Sauce (page 44), then roll up into a wrap. Serve with additional Creamy Tahini Sauce for dipping.

Kousa Mahshi: Stuffed Squash, Lebanese-Style

This is another one of those dishes that immigrants coming to the United States from Lebanon in the early 1900s tried to hold onto, and not just the dish, but also the name. In Lebanese circles today you won't hear them refer to stuffed squash. It's *Kousa Mahshi*.

Holding on to heritage is very important. Sometimes what makes us different is what brings us together. I remember when Pope Saint John Paul II wrote his encyclical *Ut Unum Sint (That They May Be One)*. At about the same time, he issued and Apostolic Letter on the Eastern Churches called *Orientale Lumen* in Latin. It means *The Light from the East*. It was in this document that Pope Saint John Paul II used the analogy of the Church needing both lungs to breathe, East and West. I was a seminarian when these documents were first published, and I had experienced at least three different Eastern rites in the Catholic Church: the Byzantine, the Maronite, and the Melkite rites. Since first attending a Maronite Rite Mass as a teenager, I have had an appreciation for the Eastern churches, including our Orthodox brothers and sisters, and I long for the day that Jesus' desire will be fulfilled and we will all be one.

Early last century, the early 1900s, was a different time. Different ethnic groups did not mingle, unless they worked together. You can see this clearly in New Orleans where, in some areas of the city, there are Catholic churches right across the street from each other. Why? Because the Germans and Irish didn't mix. Neither did the French or the Italians. Yet they were all Roman Catholics! In the work world people had to mix and mingle to do business. But when it came to faith, and food, and family, they tried to hang on to their heritage.

Imagine what it was like for Eastern Rite Catholics at that time. They were in full union with Rome, but had very different disciplines and practices than what was common in the American Catholic experience of that time. They suffered from lack of priests, from lack of cultural connection, and from misunderstandings by average Roman Catholics in America. Without their own priests and their own rites, many of the Eastern Catholics slowly became assimilated into the Latin Rite, which was the main Catholic rite in America. But now, we strive to hold onto our individual heritage and those documents written by Pope St. John Paul II have helped us better appreciate the various rites of the Church.

Kousa Mahshi is one of those traditions that has been handed down by generations of Labanese families in the US. The recipe here is our version of this classic dish. The *mahshi* (or *filling*) for this recipe is about the same as it is for the Lebanese Grape Leaves, except here we are using beef instead of lamb.

INGREDIENTS

- 18 to 24 medium yellow squash, cored (necks too)
- 5 homegrown tomatoes, chopped
- 4 cloves of garlic, crushed
- 2 pounds of ground beef
- 1 cup long-grain white rice
- Half a stick of butter, softened
- 1½ tablespoons kosher salt
- 1 tsp cayenne pepper
- Juice of one lemon

3 or 4 sprigs of fresh mint, chopped

2 quarts of beef stock or chicken stock (or water… enough to cover the squash)

Labneh (page 40) for garnish (*optional*)

INSTRUCTIONS

For the Filling
1. Combine the following ingredients in a large mixing bowl: rice, ground beef, 3 tomatoes with juice, butter, 1 tablespoon of salt, and cayenne.
2. Mix well by hand and set aside.

For the Squash
1. Wash squash well. Slice off the necks and core, leaving about ¼ inch shell. Core the necks as best as you can (a potato peeler works well for this). Rinse and drain the squash well.
2. Stuff each squash (necks too!) loosely with the filling. Arrange them in a large pot so that the open ends are facing up. Add the remaining tomatoes to the pot and sprinkle squash with the remaining salt and the chopped mint.
3. Fill pot with beef (or chicken) stock so that the squash are completely covered.
4. Bring to a hard boil, and allow to boil for a few minutes. Then reduce heat to medium, add the lemon juice, and cover. Simmer for 45 minutes.

Lamb-Stuffed Bell Peppers

It's impossible to escape the humble bell pepper in south Louisiana. The bell pepper is, after all, one of the ingredients that makes up the *trinity*. Onions and celery are the other two. Anyone from Louisiana knows that the *trinity* undergirds so many of our traditional Cajun and Creole dishes. It is unescapable indeed.

Growing up I did not like bell peppers. I remember my mother stuffing bell peppers from time to time. I ate the stuffing, and left the pepper. I thought of the bell pepper as just a "container" for the stuffing. Nothing more.

I like bell peppers now. When I make gumbo or jambalaya, I tend to add *extra* bell peppers. I don't know when that change occurred or why, but I'm glad it did. Perhaps my palate just grew up a bit. Or maybe I've just had the opportunity over the years to try bell peppers prepared (or used) in so many different ways. Whatever the reason, I now appreciate the semi-sweet green-like flavor of the bell pepper.

One of my favorite ways to prepare bell peppers (when I want to *feature* them) is to stuff them with beef, rice, tomatoes, and spices. There are many twists to stuffed bell peppers, the most popular of which—in these parts—would be Cajun or Creole. But today I especially like this Middle Eastern recipe for stuffed bell peppers. This recipe is made even more unique by the accompanying *Labneh*, in which you can dip each bite of the pepper and the stuffing.

The recipe below will yield about 10 stuffed bell peppers, depending on the size of the peppers. If you want to make a smaller batch, just halve the recipe.

INGREDIENTS

- 10 green bell peppers, tops cut off and seeds removed (reserve the tops)
- 28 oz. can of petite diced tomatoes
- 5 to 6 cloves of garlic, crushed
- 2 pounds of ground beef
- 1 cup long-grain white rice
- Half a stick of butter, softened
- 1½ tablespoons kosher salt
- 1 tsp cayenne pepper
- 1 tsp allspice (or Seven Spice, if you can find it)
- Juice of one lemon
- 3 or 4 sprigs of fresh mint, chopped (about 4 teaspoons total)
- 2 quarts of beef stock or chicken stock (or water....enough to cover the peppers)

Labneh for garnish (*optional*)

INSTRUCTIONS

For the Filling

1. Combine the following ingredients in a large mixing bowl: rice, ground beef, crushed garlic, about 14 ounces of petite diced tomatoes with juice, softened butter, 1 tablespoon of salt, and cayenne, Allspice or Seven Spice, two teaspoons of fresh mint, and the juice of one lemon.
2. Mix well by hand and set aside.

For the bell peppers

1. Wash the bell peppers well. Slice off the tops and remove the seeds.
2. Stuff each pepper loosely with the filling. Arrange them in a large pot so that the open ends are facing up. Add the remaining tomatoes to the pot and sprinkle peppers with the remaining salt and the remaining chopped mint, then

place the bell pepper tops back on the peppers. (Note: If you do not have a pot big enough, then arrange them in a large pan, cover the pan with foil and bake in a preheated oven at 350 degrees for 45 minutes to an hour).

3. Fill pot (or pan) with beef (or chicken) stock so that the peppers are almost completely covered.

4. Bring to a hard boil, and allow to boil for a few minutes. Then reduce heat to medium and cover. Simmer for 45 minutes.

NOTE: A NOTE ABOUT THE STUFFING

Like the Kousa Mahshi (or Lebanese Stuffed Squash), the mahshi for this recipe is about the same as it is for the Lebanese Grape Leaves, except here we are using beef instead of lamb. When filling the peppers, make sure you do so loosely because the rice will expand as it cooks.

Grilled Lamb Chops

Holy Thursday commemorates the Last Supper, and Jesus' institution of the Eucharist. My wife Char, our children, and I love the Easter Triduum, and Holy Thursday sets the tone for us.

We strive to celebrate the events of those three days not only through the liturgical celebrations at church, but also in our prayers and actions at home in our "domestic church."

Holy Thursday is always a special treat. Char's family is Lebanese, so we love Greek and Lebanese cuisine, including lamb. For us Holy Thursday is a celebration, a feast. We plan our supper so that we can arrive to church in time for the 7:00 p.m. Mass of the Last Supper. And what a meal we have!

Our Holy Thursday menu consists of grilled lamb chops, roasted potatoes, creamed spinach, Pita, a Romaine salad, and wine. Absolutely splendid! We come to the table in our Sunday best. We set the table with our best china and silver, with crystal goblets for the wine. We all sit together and I lead the family in prayer. Before we serve the plates, I read the story of the Passover from the Book of Exodus. There is a sense of solemnity in our dining room, and we recognize that God is with us.

Once the meal is done, in good Israelite-Passover fashion, we leave the dishes on the table and rush (with our loins girt!) to make it to church on time. The solemnity of the Mass, with its readings and its rite of washing feet, reinforces for us the fact that our family is part of a bigger family, the Family of God. Not only do we need to nourish ourselves daily with food on our kitchen table (and good food!), we also need to nourish ourselves with the best food, which is found on God's table. Our little family gathering daily around the kitchen table is an image of the Family of God gathering around the altar during Mass. And that is a beautiful thing.

INGREDIENTS

6 to 8 lamb chops

Dry Greek seasoning (oregano, rosemary, thyme, black pepper, red pepper flakes)

4 cloves of garlic

Coarse ground kosher salt

Extra virgin olive oil

INSTRUCTIONS

1. Remove lamb chops from packaging, rinse with cold water, then pat dry with paper towels. Place in a pan to marinate.
2. Coat each side of the lamb chops with olive oil.
3. Sprinkle both sides of the lamb chops with salt (to taste) and a generous amount of the Greek seasoning. Rub it in.
4. Crush 4 or 5 cloves of garlic, and sprinkle it on and around the chops.
5. Cover the dish and put in the refrigerator to marinate. Marinate for a few hours (at least 1 hour).
6. When you are ready to cook, remove the lamb from the fridge and allow to come to room temperature, about 20 to 30 minutes. Heat the grill to around 425 or 450 degrees. When heated, lay the lamb chops out on the grill. Grill them for 3 or 4 minutes on each side (depending on how cooked you prefer your lamb).

Rack of Lamb

A rack of lamb is a section of 7 or 8 lamb ribs. The classic way to prepare and present a rack of lamb is to "*french*" the meat, which exposes the bones. Frenching means to strip away the meat and fat that extends to the end of the rib bones. This technique does nothing for the taste of the meat, it's all about the presentation. You can have your butcher french the lamb for you, or you can do it yourself.

I hate the thought of wasting anything. I save the bones from chickens, and save all the unusable parts of vegetables like onions, carrots, and garlic to make my stocks. Frenching the rack of lamb, removes meat and fat, so what are you going to do with what you remove? I either save it for Lamb Stew, or I use to line my pot when making Stuffed Grape Leaves.

You can serve rack of lamb with Labneh or mint jelly, if you like. We are careful to use any kind of sauce sparingly. We don't want to take away from the taste of the lamb. You can make a simple mint sauce with fresh mint, honey, and apple cider vinegar. To give it a little kick, add some Dijon mustard. To make the sauce, add ½ cup of fresh mint leaves, 2 tablespoons of honey, and 1/3 cup of apple cider vinegar in a food processor. Pulse until the mint is minced and the sauce is well-combined. If desired, add mustard a tablespoon at a time, to taste. Pulse to incorporate the mustard.

INGREDIENTS

2 racks of lamb, frenched (about 2 pounds)

Kosher salt, to taste

Freshly cracked black pepper, to taste

Granulated garlic, to taste

4 tablespoons extra virgin olive oil

1 cup Italian bread crumbs

INSTRUCTIONS

1. Preheat oven to 350 degrees.
2. Trim off any extra fat from the racks of lamb.
3. Season to taste with the kosher salt, black pepper, and granulated garlic, and rub the seasonings in well on both sides of each rack.
4. Combine the Italian bread crumbs and the olive oil in a bowl, then cover the outside of each rack (the "fat" side, or the tops) with the olive oil and Italian bread crumb mixture.
5. In a roasting pan intermingle the two rack so they are standing up with the fat side out.
6. Place in the preheated oven and roast, uncovered, for 15 to 18 minutes.
7. Remove from oven and allow to rest for 10 minutes before cutting.

Pan-Fried Chicken
with Tomato and Feta Dressing

I love Chicken Shawarma. If I am out at a Greek or Lebanese restaurant, I have a hard time *not* ordering Chicken Shawarma. As a Chicken Shawarma aficionado, I totally lucked out our first day in Bethlehem.

After celebrating Christmas Mass in the Church of the Nativity, we traveled a short distance to visit Shepherd's Field, where the angels appeared to the shepherds and announced to them the good news of the birth of Jesus. Just down the street from Shepherd's Field there are a couple of restaurants. We had lunch at one of them. It was a Christian family-owned restaurant that specializes in… Falafel and Shawarma. Yes!

Our group was able to sample the Falafel while we waited on our Chicken Shawarma sandwiches to arrive. It was all perfect, of course, and it made me start thinking of how I could finally make Chicken Shawarma at home.

But Shawarma is not easy to make at home.

Why?

Because Chicken Shawarma is made by alternately stacking strips of chicken fat and pieces of raw seasoned chicken on a spit. In restaurants, and on street carts, a vertical spit is most typical. The chicken is roasted slowly on all sides as the spit rotates in front of a flame for hours. Traditionally, a wood fire was used, but nowadays a gas flame is most common.

Can you make this at home?

Me neither.

So what is a Shawarma lover to do?

Well, the only practical option—if you really want to make something like Chicken Shawarma at home—is to compromise and make something that is Chicken Shawarma-like. And that is exactly what this recipe attempts to do.

The flavors are there. Using chicken thighs means you retain the moistness of Shawarma. The accompanying sauce rounds out the dish. The chicken can be served on a plate and topped with the sauce, or it can all be rolled up in Arabic Bread and eaten as a sandwich.

INGREDIENTS

1 pint of grape tomatoes, halved

1/3 cup pitted Kalamata olives

4 ounces Feta cheese, coarsely crumbled

1/2 cup fresh mint leaves, minced

Half a bunch of green onions, chopped

3 tablespoons extra virgin olive oil

1–2 tablespoons regular olive oil or coconut oil

Coarse kosher salt and freshly ground black pepper, to taste

Cayenne pepper, to taste

2 pounds boneless chicken thighs, sliced in strips

INSTRUCTIONS

1. Combine tomatoes, olives, Feta, mint, green onions and 2 to 3 tablespoons of extra virgin olive oil in a glass mixing bowl. Season with salt and pepper and set aside.
2. Season chicken cutlets with salt and pepper and cayenne, to taste.
3. Heat a heavy-bottomed skillet (cast-iron or stainless) over medium-high heat. Coat with regular olive oil or coconut oil. Add cutlets to the hot skillet and cook until chicken is cooked through, about 1 to 2 minutes per side. Do so in batches, if necessary. Then, transfer chicken to a plate and cover with aluminum foil to keep warm.
4. Serve the chicken on plates. Top with the tomato mixture.

Kafta (Lamb Meatballs)

Is it Kafta, Kofta, or Kufta?

Well, it depends. I've seen it—and heard it referred to—as all three. But those three words all point to the same thing: delectable lamb.

Lamb is a favorite in our house, and not just because of the obvious scriptural references to Jesus as the Lamb of God. At large family gatherings on my wife's side the tables are usually covered with stuffed grape leaves, *kousa mahshi* (stuffed squash), Hummus, Pita (which used to be called Arabic Bread or Syrian Bread), Tabbouleh, Baba Ganoush, Labneh, different types of Kibbeh, and sometimes even lamb chops.

The difference in spelling and pronunciation of the name of this dish may have something to with its Middle Eastern origins or the fact that it's an English derivation of an Arabic word. Lamb and goat are plentiful in Lebanon, Syria, Israel, and all across the Middle East, and many lamb dishes are prepared virtually the same way in these different countries, yet they may go by different names. In fact, most of the foods in the region are basically the same. It's just that each country may have a different name for them. This is simply the result of cultural and language differences.

And when you bring this Arabic dish over to the States, then you add an entirely new culture (and language!) into the mix. Consider the Bread we refer to as Pita Bread. Originally, here in the States, it was referred to as Arabic Bread or Syrian Bread. It wasn't until the 1970s that it began to be referred to as Pita Bread. Pita is a Greek word. I believe is was back in the 1970s that Syria fell out of favor with the US. I recall reading somewhere that prior to the 1970s, Arabic Flat Bread used to be called Syrian Bread, and it was only available at local Middle Eastern markets. To keep things positive, the same Arabic Flat Bread started to be called Pita Bread even though the traditional Greek Pita Bread was much thicker.

If you want to make a Lebanese feast, with Kafta as the centerpiece, then you might want to create a menu with Hummus, Tabbouleh, and… Pita.

INGREDIENTS

2 pounds ground lamb (beef ground round can be substituted)

1 large sweet yellow onion, finely chopped

4 cloves of garlic, well crushed with a mortar & pestle (or just minced)

6 tablespoons of fresh parsley, chopped

2 tablespoons of fresh mint, chopped

1 teaspoon freshly cracked black pepper

2 teaspoons of kosher salt

½ teaspoon cayenne pepper, or to taste

1 teaspoon allspice

1 teaspoon cinnamon

1 teaspoon cumin

INSTRUCTIONS

1. Preheat grill or oven to medium-high heat. If you are cooking them in the oven, then set it to Broil.
2. Mix all ingredients together. Wrap mixture around metal skewers.
3. Cook on the grill or broil in the oven, turning at least once for even cooking. Cook time depends on heat of the grill or oven and the thickness of the kabobs.

NOTE: ALTERNATIVES
The meat can also be rolled into meatballs and browned in a hot skillet for use in other recipes.

Baked Kibbeh

Kibbeh is essentially a dish made with beef, lamb, or goat and cracked wheat (bulgur wheat). It is usually seasoned with minced onions, salt, cayenne, and a traditional Middle Eastern spice such as cinnamon, cumin or allspice. Kibbeh comes in different forms. You can find it baked like a casserole, fried as football-shaped croquettes, or even served raw with olive oil and a little mint.

Yes, I said *raw*.

Kibbeh Nayeh, or raw Kibbeh, is a Lebanese delicacy served with warm Pita. Though it can be made with beef or goat, I have most frequently seen it made with lamb. The meat is combined with all the elements of Kibbeh listed above and then presented as a mound on a plate, with the shape of a cross indented on the top of the mound. The whole thing is drizzled with olive oil. In our house we like to make the cross and fill it with olive oil.

Since Kibbeh Nayeh is eaten raw, freshness is of paramount importance. In the old country, Kibbeh Nayeh was made the same day the sheep or goat was slaughtered, and that guaranteed its freshness. Today, you would go to a trusted butcher for the lamb, and you would usually have to place your order for it a day or two in advance. Why? Because you want the butcher to use clean blades to prevent cross-contamination with other meat. The meat for the Kibbeh Nayeh is finely ground, passing through the grinder twice, after having all fat and gristle removed.

Baked Kibbeh is a layered dish that is baked like a casserole. The top and bottom layers are the same, and the middle layer—the stuffing—is also made with lamb and bulgur wheat, but it's cooked beforehand with finely chopped onions, toasted pine nuts, and spices. So, before baking, you end up with a layer of raw Kibbeh, topped with a layer of cooked Kibbeh, topped with a layer of raw Kibbeh. The end result is that the middle layer will have a different consistency than the top and bottom layers, but they all bind together when baking.

Oh, and the whole dish is topped with melted butter.

INGREDIENTS

For the Outer Layers:

2 pounds. finely ground lamb, not lean (can substitute beef, eye of round works well)

2 cups bulgur wheat (#1 grade)

1 large sweet yellow onion, grated (or pulsed finely in a food processor)

5 teaspoons kosher salt, or to taste

1 teaspoon freshly cracked black pepper

½ teaspoon cayenne

1 tablespoon cinnamon

1 tablespoon allspice

For the Stuffing:

1 pound. ground lamb, not lean (can substitute ground beef, chuck)

1 medium sweet yellow onion, finely chopped

½ cup pine nuts, toasted

1 teaspoon kosher salt, or to taste

½ teaspoon freshly cracked black pepper, or to taste

¼ teaspoon cayenne

½ teaspoon cinnamon

½ teaspoon allspice

2 tablespoons butter

Juice of ½ to 1 lemon

INSTRUCTIONS

Make the stuffing:

1. In a skillet over medium-high heat, add the butter, the onions, and a dash of salt. Sauté until the onions are soft.
2. Add the meat, the rest of the salt, the pepper, cayenne, cinnamon, and allspice. Mix well to incorporate, and cook until the meat is browned. Make sure to break up the meat as much as possible as it cooks.
3. Once browned, add lemon juice and stir in. Taste and adjust seasoning as needed.

Make the Kibbeh for the outer layers:

1. Place the bulgur wheat in a fine mesh sieve and rinse under cold water. Transfer it to a glass bowl and cover with enough water to submerge the bulgur by at least a ½ inch. Allow it to soak for at least 30 to 45 minutes. Drain and grab handfuls at a time, squeezing as much water out as you can, and transfer to a large mixing bowl.
2. Add the meat, along with the onion and the spices, and knead it with your hands until thoroughly incorporated. You'll need to dip your hands in cold water as you work with the meat to prevent it from sticking, and to help soften the Kibbeh.
3. The Kibbeh should have a very fine consistency. If it is still too chunky, you can pulse it—in batches—in a food processor.

Assembling the Baked Kibbeh:

1. Preheat your oven to 400 degrees.
2. Using your hands, coat bottom and sides of a 9 x 12 inch baking dish with butter.
3. With a bowl of cold water handy, evenly spread half of the Kibbeh on the bottom of the pan, dipping your hands in cold water as you work. The bottom layer should be about ½ inch thick.
4. Spread the stuffing evenly over the bottom layer.
5. Form the top layer with the remaining Kibbeh in the same why that you did the bottom layer. Smooth out the top layer to make it even.
6. Score the top layer with a sharp knife to about a ½ inch deep, making sure you don't cut into the bottom layer. Traditionally, the top layer is scored in 1-inch diamond shapes, but you can be as creative as you want.
7. Place a small slice of butter on each square. Alternatively, you can melt ½ cup of butter and pour over the Kibbeh.
8. Place the baking dish in the oven, uncovered, and bake until golden brown and the top starts to get crispy, about 50 minutes.

Fried Kibbeh

The best-known variety of Kibbeh is the fried "football-shaped" croquette stuffed with mined beef or lamb. Although they can be served as a main course, they are often served as part of a Mezze or as an appetizer. Oh, and did I mentioned that croquettes are fried?

Here's another confession: I love fried food! I know. It's not the healthiest food to eat, but it's probably the most scrumptious, if it is fried correctly. Besides, fried food reminds me of my childhood.

My maternal grandfather, along with one of my uncles, was an avid fisherman. They were both sheriff deputies. They both lived next door to each other, and there was a stocked fishing pond just up the road. They fished other places too, but I think that pond provided more frequent opportunities to relax, and to catch fish. Every few weeks during the summer months the family got together for an old-fashioned fish fry. My grandfather and uncle would fry fish and French fries outside in the shade. They fried the fish in batches, so every once and while we made sure to run past and grab a piece of fish to tide us over until it was officially lunch time. Those were good times, but, I have to admit that I really don't fry that often at home. Every once and a while I'll fry fish or onion rings. Sometimes I'll fry Falafel. But when I do, I prefer to fry outside on propane burners. Frying outside makes for easier clean-up, and you don't have to worry about the fried food smell that can linger in your house for days.

Like Falafel, Fried Kibbeh can be served as a main course, but it is frequently served as an appetizer or as part of a Mezze. This is a great dish for parties or large family gatherings because fried Kibbeh is an excellent finger food. It's easy to carry and eat while you mix and mingle. Fried Kibbeh can be served with Labneh or Tahini Sauce for dipping.

INGREDIENTS

For the Stuffing
1 pound of ground lamb or ground beef, or a ground lamb and beef combination

1 medium sweet yellow onion, chopped

1 tablespoon extra virgin olive oil

2 teaspoons kosher salt

½ teaspoon freshly cracked black pepper, to taste

1 teaspoon allspice

1 teaspoon cinnamon

1 cup of fried pine nuts

For the Shell
2 cups fine bulgur wheat (#1 grade)

2 pounds finely ground lamb or eye of round beef

1 medium sweet yellow onion, chopped

1 tablespoon cinnamon

1 teaspoon cayenne

3 teaspoons kosher salt

Freshly cracked black pepper, to taste

1 teaspoon paprika

1 teaspoon cumin

Zest of 1 lemon

Mint leaves, as garnish

INSTRUCTIONS

For the Stuffing
1. For the stuffing, heat olive oil in a skillet over medium heat. Add the onion and cook, stirring occasionally, until soft, about 8 to 10 minutes.

2. Add the ground lamb or beef, breaking it up with a wooden spoon or spatula, and cook until no longer pink, about 8 minutes.
3. Add the seasonings….the salt, pepper, allspice, and cinnamon, and continue to cook for another 5 minutes, until the meat begins to brown.
4. Remove from heat and transfer to a bowl to cool.

For the Shell

1. Rinse the bulgur wheat and squeeze out any excess water. Place the wheat in a large bowl. Add the salt, allspice, cinnamon, black pepper, cayenne, paprika, cumin, lemon zest, and onion, along with the finely ground meat. Knead the mixture in the bowl until it becomes a paste, about 5 minutes. Cover the bowl with a clean moist dish towel to prevent the mixture from drying out.
2. Keeping your hands wet with water as you work, shape about a ¼ cup of the meat-bulgur mixture into a ball. Hold the ball in one hand and insert your index finger into the center to form a hole. Shape the ball into a thin-walled oval (about ¼-inch thick) with an opening at one end (like half a football).
3. Add 1 ½ to 2 tablespoons of the filling. Wet the edges of the opening and close it off, tapering it to match the other side, until you have a whole "football." Place it on a sheet or a dish and cover to keep from drying out. Repeat the process with the remaining mixtures.
4. Pour oil into a deep skillet or dutch oven and heat over medium heat. You are looking to get the oil to 375 degrees. You can check the temperature with a kitchen thermometer. Fry the Kibbeh balls in batches until brown all over, about 4 or 5 minutes.
5. Remove from oil with a slotted spoon and drain on paper towels.
6. Transfer to a serving platter. Serve hot with Labneh or Tahini Sauce. Garnish with fresh mint leaves.

Makloubeh

A couple of years ago I had lunch with a friend of mine at a Middle Eastern restaurant in New Orleans. It wasn't billed as a Lebanese restaurant, but I recognized all the dishes on the menu except one: Makloubeh. This was before I journeyed to the Holy Land, and it was the first time I had ever heard of Makloubeh. My friend explained it was the famous "upside down" rice dish from the Middle East. That meant nothing to me at the time. When his plate came out, I didn't see anything upside-down about it. It looked like jambalaya to me.

The first time I actually tasted Makloubeh was not in Palestine, even though this is a traditional Palestinian dish. In Jerusalem there is a restaurant called The Eucalyptus which is owned and operated by Chef Moshe Basson, a member of Chefs for Peace. During our pilgrimage we were able to eat there and for the entree Chef Moshe prepared Makloubeh.

When it was time for the entree to be served, two servers carried two large platters into the dining room, and Chef Moshe approached me with an apron to join in the presentation. I followed his lead as we carefully worked to flip the huge pot over, upside-down (we had placed a large serving platter on top of it). Then Chef Moshe directed me to wave my hand a few times over the pot in a circular motion and utter the "magic" word... For my finale Chef Moshe told me to bang my hand on the bottom of the pot. Then, together, we lifted the huge pot off of the contents, leaving the Makloubeh on the large serving platter. It was a beautiful, delicious crowd pleaser.

When making Makloubeh some families use either eggplant or cauliflower, bone-in chicken or lamb. For this recipe I used all of the above! This recipe would be great for a large dinner party of family gathering.

INGREDIENTS

4 cups long grain white, Jasmine or Basmati rice

2 pounds of ground lamb

3 or 4 pounds of bone-in chicken thighs or drumsticks

2 large sweet yellow onions, chopped

2 medium eggplant, sliced into ½ inch slices and roasted (see page 94)

1 large cauliflower, cut into florets and roasted (see page 120)

3 beefsteak tomatoes, sliced into ¼-inch slices

8 to 10 cloves of garlic, crushed

Kosher salt to taste

½ teaspoon of freshly cracked black pepper

½ teaspoon cayenne

1 teaspoon allspice

1 teaspoon cinnamon

1 teaspoon nutmeg

½ teaspoon cardamom

6½ cups of beef or chicken stock

¼ cup pomegranate molasses

Olive oil for frying

½ cup of pine nuts, toasted

½ cup of slivered almonds, toasted

See photos on page 133

INSTRUCTIONS

1. Prep and roast the eggplant and the cauliflower (see pages 94 and 120).
2. Season, to taste, with salt and black pepper, the chicken thighs and / or legs and roast them in the oven until almost fully cooked, about 40 minutes at 350, depending on the size of the pieces.
3. In a small glass bowl, combine the salt, black pepper, cayenne, allspice, cinnamon, nutmeg, and cardamom. Stir together to blend well.
4. Place the stock in a pot and bring to a simmer. Note: You will later turn the heat up so that the stock is boiling when you add it to the pot of Makloubeh.
5. Sauté the onions in butter until soft, about 10 minutes. Add garlic and sauté for an additional minute, stirring frequently to prevent the garlic from burning. Add the ground lamb and the spices, stir well and brown the lamb, then remove from heat. (Optionally, you can brown the lamb then drain before adding the seasoning.)
6. In a large pot (7 to 8 quarts), begin to "construct" the Makloubeh, keeping in mind that the pot will be flipped upside-down when served. Add enough of the rice to barely cover the bottom of the pot, then begin layering the roasted eggplant slices, followed by a layer of tomatoes. Add more rice to make a thin layer on top of the tomatoes, then add the ground lamb and onion mixture. Next add the rest of the rice, followed by the cauliflower and chicken.
7. Slowly add the boiling stock to the pot of Makloubeh along with the pomegranate molasses. Place the pot on a hot burner set to high heat. Bring the pot back to a boil, then cover and reduce heat to low. Simmer until the rice is fully cooked, 20 to 30 minutes. If the rice seems undercooked, add more stock, 1/2 cup at a time, until the rice is cooked.
8. When done, remove from heat and allow to sit for about 10 minutes before serving.
9. To serve, remove cover, place a large flat platter on top of the pot. Carefully flip the pot over so that the contents are resting on the platter. Gently remove the pot and serve.

NOTE:

For this recipe you need a large enough pot to handle the volume of ingredients and that won't spill over when you bring the stock to a boil. The pot also need to have a flat top. You don't want the handles to protrude past the top, otherwise you will have trouble flipping the pot over onto the platter.

Fish Entrees

Saint Peter's Fish, see page 158

Saint Peter's Fish (Traditional Preparation)

Located in Migdal, the hometown of Mary Magdalene, and overlooking the Sea of Galilee, Magdalena Restaurant is one of the few restaurants in the area that is owned by an Arab Christian family. And that is important.

The number of Arab Christian families (mainly Catholic and Orthodox) in The Holy Land is dwindling, particularly in Palestine where only 3 percent of the population is Christian. An important part of making a pilgrimage to the Holy Land is to try to support the local Christian families. Without them, there would be no Christian presence in the Holy Land. But being a Christian family-owned restaurant is not the only reason that Magdalena stood out to me. No. Both the atmosphere and the food were exquisite. Magdalena serves upscale Arabic cuisine with flavorful influences from Chef Joseph Hanna's Lebanese heritage. Chef Joseph Hanna sees Magdalena as a unique concept. He makes Galilee-style Arabic food, and incorporates his Lebanese and Mediterranean heritages. He takes traditional Galilee-style food and turns it into contemporary gourmet food, using mostly local ingredients that are in season. Magdalena Restaurant has been called the first Arab-gourmet restaurant in the country. And we got to dine there!

Our lunch at Magdalena followed a mid-morning boat ride on the Sea of Galilee. As part of the Food Meets Faith pilgrimage, our lunch at Magdalena was planned. Part of that lunch was supposed to be a demonstration of how they traditionally make Saint Peter's Fish. However, it was not feasible to have the entire group go back into the kitchen. Instead, Chef Joseph invited me back to the kitchen to see how the whole tilapia is prepared. What happened next was a happy surprise.

When we got to the work station, there were about 20 whole tilapia—separated four to a tray—that had been gutted, scaled, and scored, waiting to be prepped. Chef Joseph's colleague, Chef Ahmed Okla, demonstrated how they prepared the fish, as Chef Joseph called for a chef's apron to be put on me. The first thing that Chef Ahmed did was to liberally salt the inside and the outside of the fish. He followed the salt with coarse-ground black pepper, and then pulled into view a white container with what looked like Tabbouleh inside. I said, "Hey, that's Tabbouleh! That looks just like the way we make it at home!" Chef Joseph's face lit up and we started laughing. It was like we were little kids. He was so excited to show me all the different things in his kitchen, the different lettuces and greens, the herbs they use for seasoning… and we tasted everything. I was just eating it all up. Figuratively, I mean. Thankfully, our guide Arlette was there to document it all in photographs. I was having a ball.

Then Chef Ahmed turned to me and said, "OK. Now it's your turn." And he pointed to the remaining 19 fish. I smiled and got to work. In the end, I prepared the Saint Peter's Fish for everyone in my group, except for myself. Chef Joseph wanted to prepare mine.

There is something sacramental in the sharing of a meal. And in the preparation of that meal. Magdalena Restaurant wasn't a church or a holy spot, but for me, cooking and dining there was definitely a spiritual experience. Making new friends, sharing a meal around the table, enjoying the goodness of God's providence in the form of good food and good wine, was a very real experience of the family of God and of God's presence with us. Our lunch at Magdalena was a much-needed pause before making our journey to Jerusalem. We had been in The Holy Land for only three days, and only in the northern part: Natanya, Cana, Nazereth, and the area around the Sea of Galilee. Our lunch at Magdalena provided the perfect respite before our travels the following day to the Dead Sea and then on to Jerusalem.

The recipe that I share with you here is the one I got from Chef Joseph and Chef Ahmed, which follows the traditional way to prepare Saint Peter's Fish. It calls for whole tilapia. If you can't get whole tilapia, you could substitute tilapia fillets, using the sauce as a marinade and a topping. You would need to reduce the cook time to about 15 to 20 minutes, or until the fish flakes. The marinade can be made in advance and stored in the refrigerator for a couple of days before use.

INGREDIENTS

½ cup extra-virgin olive oil

1 to 2 bunches of fresh Italian flat leaf parsley, finely chopped

2 to 4 tablespoons fresh mint, finely chopped

1 bunch green onions, finely chopped

1 sweet yellow onion, finely chopped

6-8 medium vine tomatoes, diced

The juice of 1 to 2 lemons

1 teaspoon kosher salt, or to taste, plus additional to season each fish

½ to 1 teaspoon cayenne pepper, or to taste

Freshly cracked black pepper, to taste, to season each fish

4 or 5 whole tilapia, gutted, scaled and scored 3 times on each side

4 or 5 large sprigs of rosemary

INSTRUCTIONS

1. Chop and dice the parsley, mint, onion, green onion, and tomato and place all in a large glass bowl.
2. Add the ½ cup of extra-virgin olive oil and lemon juice to the bowl and mix well. It's best to go slowly. This is one of those "you gotta eyeball it" recipes. There are lots of variables: the size of the bunches of parsley, the size of the bunch of green onions, etc. It takes practice (and lots of tasting!) to get it just right. So go slow on the olive oil and the lemon juice. Then season with salt and cayenne to taste.
3. Cover with plastic wrap and refrigerate for at least an hour for the flavors to marry.
4. Take a tilapia and season generously inside and out (and both sides) with salt and black pepper, making sure that you season inside the scoring marks too. Using a large serving spoon, scoop a generous amount of the marinade into the cavity of the fish, then add more marinade to the top of the fish, working it into the score marks with your hands. Finally, add some of the rosemary to the fish, inside and out.
5. Repeat this process with the remaining fish.
6. Place fish on a large baking tray and bake in the oven at 400 degrees for 30 minutes or until fish flakes.

Serve alongside roasted vegetables and a salad.

See photo on page 157

Mediterranean Trout

Speckled Trout is plentiful in the waters of Louisiana, and as a result, you will find trout prominently listed on restaurant menus throughout the state. Whether it's fried trout, Trout Amandine, Trout Meuniere, or even Barbecued Trout, this fish makes happy eaters and happy people.

Louisiana is called the Sportsman's Paradise because of the abundance of hunting and fishing available. As a matter of fact, fishing and shrimping are major industries in the state. I grew up eating fresh catfish, trout, bream, crawfish, shrimp, and crabs. I looked forward to Fridays in Lent because I knew my mom would be frying fish or shrimp, and her famous "Sandy Fries." I can still see my dad walking in the house with fresh shrimp or fish wrapped tightly in newspaper, a "catch" he probably scored from one of the many street vendors on the side of the road in Baton Rouge.

When I started to take my faith seriously, around the age of 16, I wanted to really practice my faith and live out the call to fasting, abstinence, and conversion during Lent. This proved problematic because of the plethora of Friday fish fries in parishes across the south. The good Knights of Columbus always seemed to couple good cooking with their good works, which is kind of how Jesus did it: *If you feed them, they will come.* In the later part of my teenage years, I struggled with this. Youth can indeed be idealistic, and I had a hard time reconciling the church-endorsed feasting with the liturgical celebration of Lent. Now that I am older, I understand that the good work of the Knights is funded in large part by fundraising activities like the Friday fish fries. I also now understand that I have the power of choice. I can choose to eat lightly. No one forces me to feast of fish and shrimp on Fridays in Lent.

Frying is not the only way to cook fish, of course. This recipe, for example, is different from what you would typically find in my neck of the woods. It has more of a Greek/Mediterranean flavor profile, and it is winner. You can use white or yellow onions, but if you are like me and enjoy bigger bites of onion, then just halving or quartering the pearl onions might work best for you.

INGREDIENTS

4 trout fillets

Kosher salt, to taste

Freshly cracked black pepper, to taste

1 tablespoon small capers

2 tablespoons green olives, pitted and chopped

10 pearl onions, chopped

1 pound ripe plum tomatoes, chopped (you can substitute 1-28 oz. can of petite diced tomatoes)

½ bunch of fresh parsley, chopped

2 cloves of garlic, minced

1 cup dry white wine

3 tablespoons extra virgin olive oil

Juice of half a lemon

INSTRUCTIONS

1. Preheat oven to 425 degrees.
2. Grease a baking dish with the olive oil, and place the trout in the dish and season them with salt.
3. In a bowl, combine the capers, olives, onion, tomatoes, garlic, lemon juice, and parsley. Mix well and pour over the trout.
4. Pour wine over the trout. Drizzle with olive oil and season with salt and pepper.
5. Bake until the trout are just cooked through, about 20 minutes.

Garlic Shrimp
with Tomatoes, Peppers, and Feta

Each Memorial Day weekend in May you can find us in one place: the Greek Festival at Holy Trinity Greek Orthodox Cathedral in New Orleans. This has been a "family" tradition since before my wife and I were married...that's been over 15 years now.

One of our favorite things about the Greek Fest every year is the Greek grocery. Kalamata olives, dried Greek spices, Greek olive oils, handmade Greek Pita Bread, and handmade Greek cheeses are available for sale in the grocery all weekend. Every year we stock up on our favorite Greek cheese: Feta. When I say "stock up," I mean we usually buy three to five pounds of Feta cheese to bring home. At $5.00 per pound, that's a really good deal! Unfortunately—no matter how much of it we seem to buy—it never lasts as long as we think it will. Greek Fest is not the only exciting thing that happens in May. The Louisiana spring shrimp season usually starts in April or May, and fresh shrimp are always plentiful in June and July.

Those two events—Greek Fest and the opening of shrimp season—are the inspiration behind this simple and delicious recipe: Garlic Shrimp with Tomatoes, Peppers, and Feta. It could be said that this dish is related to Shrimp Creole, but there is less of a red sauce (or "red gravy" if you are from New Orleans) in this dish. Both, however, are served over rice.

INGREDIENTS

2 pounds large or jumbo shrimp, peeled and deveined

4 tablespoons extra-virgin olive oil

6 cloves of garlic, minced

Zest from 1 lemon

Coarse-ground Kosher salt, to taste

Freshly ground black pepper, to taste

Cayenne, to taste

1 medium to large Vidalia onion, chopped

1 green bell pepper, seeded and chopped

1 red bell pepper, seeded and chopped

1 teaspoon red pepper flakes

3 to 4 Creole (or homegrown) tomatoes, peeled and chopped (reserve juice)

¼ cup dry white wine

4 tablespoons chopped fresh parsley

About 8 ounces of Feta cheese, crumbled

3 to 4 tablespoons Ouzo (optional). Ouzo is the anise-flavored aperitif of Greece. It adds a distinctly Greek flavor to this dish.

If you opt to use Ouzo, you can add 1 tablespoon to the marinade, and 2 to 3 tablespoons to the sauce when you add the tomatoes and wine).

INSTRUCTIONS

1. In a medium-sized glass mixing bowl, add the shrimp, 1-2 tablespoons of olive oil, 1-2 teaspoons of garlic, the lemon zest, ½ teaspoon of salt, ¼ teaspoon of black pepper, and 1/8 teaspoon of cayenne. Mix well. Then set aside.

2. Heat a large heavy-bottomed skillet over medium to medium-high heat. Add 2 to 3 tablespoons of olive oil. After a minute, when the oil is hot, add the onion and red and green bell peppers. Sprinkle with a dash of salt and give it a good stir. Sauté until the vegetables have softened, about 10 minutes, stirring occasionally.

3. Add the remaining garlic and the red pepper flakes, and continue to sauté until the garlic softens, about 2 minutes. You will need to stir more frequently at this point.

4. Add the tomatoes and reserved juice and the white wine. Increase heat to medium-high if you started out at medium, and bring to a simmer. Then reduce the heat

to medium and simmer for about 8 to 10 minutes, stirring occasionally. At this point, you really want the flavors to marry and for the sauce to thicken just a bit. Stir in 2 tablespoons of the parsley and season the sauce with salt and pepper to taste.

5. Reduce the heat to medium-low and add the shrimp and marinade to the sauce. Stir to mix well, making sure the shrimp level out so they cook evenly. Simmer, stirring occasionally, until the shrimp are cooked through, about 7 to 9 minutes. You might need to extend that time a couple of minutes if you are using jumbo shrimp.

6. Remove from heat and top with crumbled Feta (some of the crumbled Feta will melt and add a creaminess to the sauce, but most of it will remain intact and add a delightful tanginess). Serve immediately over rice. Drizzle with olive oil and garnish with a generous pinch of parsley.

NOTE: PEELING TOMATOES

Peeling the tomatoes is not absolutely essential. The main reason you would want to do that is to avoid having those pesky, stringy tomato skins in your sauce. It doesn't impact the flavor at all, but peeling the tomatoes will make eating this dish a more delightful experience. To peel the tomatoes, score the skins on the top of the tomato by gently running a sharp knife through the skin making an X across the top. Bring a pot of water to a boil. One at a time, gently drop each tomato into the boiling water with a slotted spoon. Retrieve each tomato after 10 to 15 seconds and place into a bowl of ice water. Once the tomatoes cool to where you can handle them, simple peel off and discard the skins.

Eggplant and Shrimp Casserole

My daughters tell me that they don't like the word *casserole*. It sounds old-fashioned and boring, they say. Not this casserole. It's far from being boring. As a matter of fact, it pops with flavor!

A casserole is essentially a one-pot meal cooked slowly in an oven. It can be cooked in a pot or a large skillet, but most often you would use a casserole dish. I'm a big fan of one-pot meals. As a matter of fact, many of our favorite traditional Creole and Cajun dishes are one-pot meals: gumbo, jambalaya, étouffée, red beans and rice…these are all one-pot meals. One-pot meals exist to save time and to feed a crowd.

Take Red Beans and Rice as an example. In south Louisiana, Mondays are Red Beans and Rice days. Restaurants all across south Louisiana will have Red Beans and Rice on their menus on Mondays. Why? Because Mondays used to be wash day. The women were busy doing laundry all day, and didn't have time to cook. So they put on a pot of beans, turned the stove on low, and let them cook all day. When the wash was done, they might throw in some sausage to spice the beans up a bit, but essentially they had a full meal ready to be eaten. There's nothing quite like those creamy red beans after they've been cooking for hours on low heat! Red Beans and Rice are a big deal down here. Famous jazz musician Louis Armstrong used to sign all his letters "*Red Beans & Ricely Yours.*" Don't you just love that?

One-pot meals save time and feed a crowd. It's the same with this casserole. The recipe calls for the casserole to cook in the oven for 45 minutes at 375 degrees. You could certainly lower the temperature and cook it for a longer time, if you need to. I like to add a little extra cayenne because we like things spicy. Slow-cooking this casserole yields eggplant that will melt in your mouth like butter, while the shrimp retain their soft yet firm texture.

INGREDIENTS

3 medium eggplants, peeled and cubed

1 pound shrimp, peeled and cut into 1-inch pieces

1 sweet yellow onion, chopped

½ green bell pepper, chopped

3 cloves of garlic, minced

¼ cup of extra virgin olive oil (some of this will be used to grease the casserole dish)

1 ½ teaspoon kosher salt, or to taste

½ teaspoon freshly cracked black pepper

½ teaspoon cayenne

½ teaspoon thyme

½ teaspoon oregano

1 cup Panko bread crumbs

½ bunch of fresh parsley, chopped

INSTRUCTIONS

1. Preheat the oven to 375 degrees.
2. Peel and cube the eggplants, then boil until tender. Drain and set aside.
3. In a large skillet over medium-high heat, sauté the onion and bell pepper in olive oil until softened.
4. Add the garlic and the shrimp and sauté, stirring frequently, until the shrimp turn pink, about 2 to 3 minutes.
5. Add the eggplant to the skillet and mash it while stirring to incorporate.
6. Stir in the salt, pepper, cayenne, thyme, oregano, bread crumbs, and parsley. Mix well to incorporate and allow to cook for another minute or two.

7. Meanwhile, grease a casserole dish with olive oil.

7b. If you don't mind mixing cheese with seafood, then you can add a about a ½ cup of Parmesan (or even crumbled Feta) to the mixture just before transferring it to the casserole dish.

8. Transfer the mixture to the casserole dish and bake at 375 degrees for about 45 minutes, until bubbly and golden brown.

Spicy Baked Tilapia Fillets

As noted earlier, Tilapia are the fish Peter and Andrew, and James and John used to catch on the Sea of Galilee. It's the same fish Jesus cooked on the beach over a charcoal fire after his resurrection. They are still harvested from the Sea of Galilee today.

Thanks to the method of fish farming, Tilapia are also plentiful in the United States. The ones I've seen at home appear to be smaller than the ones in the Holy Land, but they are an excellent fish to cook. Tilapia is a firm white fish, and it can hold its own in recipes that would make other fish crumble to pieces. Whenever I make Fish Tacos (recipe available at CatholicFoodie.com), I use Tilapia. I can pan-fry it or broil it and it will retain its shape. It will stay together, even when wrapped in a corn or flour tortilla and topped with salsa and pickled cabbage. Yum!

This recipe—Spicy Baked Tilapia Fillets—is quick and easy to make. If you aren't a fan of spicy foods, you could just omit the cayenne. Dredging and battering the fillets before baking them will yield a slightly crunchy crust on the outside, while inside the fish becomes tender and flaky. I enjoy a squeeze of lemon on most fried or baked fish, but that is optional. I also find this fish enhanced by a drizzle of Tahini Cream Sauce.

INGREDIENTS

4 tilapia fillets

2 cups Panko bread crumbs

4 tablespoons shredded Parmesan cheese

1 teaspoon kosher salt

1 teaspoon cayenne

2 tablespoons whole milk

1 egg

Olive oil or butter

Lemon wedges, as garnish

Creamy Tahini Sauce, as garnish

INSTRUCTIONS

1. Preheat oven to 400 degrees.
2. Coat baking pan with olive oil or butter.
3. In a mixing bowl, combine the Panko bread crumbs, salt, cayenne, and Parmesan cheese and mix together well.
4. In a shallow bowl whisk together the egg and milk.
5. Dredge each fillet—one at a time—in the egg and milk mixture, then transfer to a clean work surface like a large plate, and coat both sides with the bread crumbs mixture. Place in the baking pan. Repeat this process for each fillet.
6. Place the baking pan in the oven and bake until the fish flakes easily with the fork, about 14 to 15 minutes.
7. Serve on plates with fresh lemon wedges. You can also drizzle Creamy Tahini Sauce over the fillets.

Trout with Pistachios and Dill

It's kind of funny that my only real work experience in a restaurant was as a bartender. I started out as a bartender at Drusilla Seafood Restaurant in Baton Rouge, and I tended bar for five years before entering the seminary (for the second time). I remember having dinner with then-Bishop Alfred Hughes, who was the bishop of Baton Rouge at the time. He asked me about my experience as a bartender, noting that it seemed an unusual leap—from bartender to priest. I chuckled and said, "Actually, Bishop, there are a lot of similarities between a bartender and a priest. I can't tell you how many confessions I have heard." He started to laugh. "But, you will be happy to know that I have never given absolution, only Absolute."

Not only was Drusilla Seafood the place where I first met my wife, but it also gave me a great education in preparing seafood dishes. Two of the most popular dishes at Drusilla were Trout Meuniere and Trout Amandine. Trout Amandine is the inspiration behind this recipe. Speckled Trout is plentiful in south Louisiana, but you can use any firm white fish like grouper or tilapia. The pistachios and dill go well together, and pan-frying the fish makes for a beautiful presentation.

INGREDIENTS

½ cup milk

½ cup flour

1 teaspoon Cajun or Creole spices such as Tony Chachere's or Konriko

½ teaspoon allspice

Salt, to taste

Freshly cracked black pepper, to taste

4 tablespoons butter, plus 4 additional tablespoons to sauté the pistachios

½ cup roughly chopped pistachios

5 or 6 skinless trout fillets

Juice of 1 lemon

2 tablespoons fresh dill

INSTRUCTIONS

1. Rinse the trout fillets and pat dry with paper towels. Set aside.
2. Combine flour, Cajun or Creole seasoning, and allspice in a wide plate or other dish. Stir well to combine.
3. Pour milk into a wide high-rimmed plate or other dish.
4. Season the fish fillets with salt and pepper to taste. Use your hands to gently pat the seasonings into the fish, then dip the fillets into the milk and dredge them in the seasoned flour to coat.
5. Melt 4 tablespoons of butter in a large skillet over medium to medium-high heat. Add the fillets in batches, but be careful not to overcrowd the skillet. Cook on each side until golden brown, about 3 minutes per side, then transfer to a serving platter. Repeat this process with the remaining batches, adding a little more butter if necessary.
6. Add the remaining 4 tablespoons of butter to the skillet over medium-high heat. Holding the skillet over the heat (over the burner, but not on it) gently swirl the skillet around so that the butter melts evenly. Continue to cook the butter until the it starts to turn brown, about 5 minutes. Reduce the heat to medium-low, place the skillet back on the burner and add the pistachios. Cook, stirring gently, until the pistachios are toasted, about 2 to 3 minutes. Add the lemon juice and dill, then spoon the browned butter and pistachios over the fish and serve.

Baked Fish Kibbeh

This fish dish is something you won't see every day. Remember what I told you about Kibbeh earlier? Well, forget that. At least as it pertains to this recipe.

This Kibbeh is made from fish, and it originates in the northern part of Lebanon, in a city called Tripoli on the coast of the Mediterranean Sea. It's perfect for Louisiana, though, with our abundance of rivers, streams, and lakes. And the Gulf of Mexico, of course. Seafood is plentiful in Louisiana, and the Cajuns have a history of using whatever they have on hand to come up with tasty crowd-pleasing dishes. It should be no surprise, then, that I first encountered this recipe in a locally made cookbook of Lebanese cuisine that saw only a short run in the Baton Rouge area in the 1970s.

I guess my earlier definition of Kibbeh still fits if you consider that you are using the meat of the fish together with bulgur wheat. Like a Baked Kibbeh of beef or lamb, this Fish Kibbeh also has a top and bottom layer that enclose a layer of stuffing. The citrus is used to enhance the flavor of the fish, while the egg is used as a binding agent. There's not much fat in fish, so you need something to hold it all together, and an egg works well. You will also want to use a firm white fish, like Tilapia.

INGREDIENTS

For the Kibbeh

3 pounds tilapia fillets

2 cups fine bulgur wheat (#1 grade)

½ orange peel

½ lemon peel

1 egg

1 small sweet yellow onion, finely chopped

¼ cup cilantro, chopped

2 teaspoons kosher salt

½ teaspoon freshly cracked black pepper

½ teaspoon cayenne

½ teaspoon cumin

½ teaspoon cinnamon

1 teaspoon allspice

For the Mahshi (Stuffing)

½ pound tilapia fillets

½ stick of butter

3 large sweet yellow onions, finely chopped

¼ cup pine nuts

Salt, black pepper, and allspice, to taste

INSTRUCTIONS

For the Kibbeh

1. Soak the bulgur wheat in a bowl of water for about 30 minutes.
2. Remove the bulgur wheat from water, squeezing it dry by hand to remove as much water as possible. Put it in a large mixing bowl.
3. Add the seasonings and small finely chopped onion to the wheat and mix thoroughly.
4. Place the orange and lemon peels in a food processor and pulse until chopped. Add the tilapia fillets and the cilantro to the food processor and pulse just enough to grind it all together.
5. Add the wheat mixture to the food processor and pulse to mix thoroughly into a paste that holds together well.
6. Remove the Kibbeh from the food processor and place it in a large bowl or dish. Divide it in half.

For the Mahshi (Stuffing)

1. In a large skillet over medium-high heat, sauté the onions until they begin to brown.
2. Add the pine nuts, the salt, pepper, and allspice. Stir to combine.
3. Add the tilapia fillet and sauté until fully cooked. Remove skillet from heat. Break fish up and stir to combine.

Putting It All Together

1. Preheat the oven to 350 degrees.
2. Use butter to grease a 10 x 12 baking pan. Spread half of the Kibbeh mixture in bottom of the pan.
3. Add the stuffing mixture to the pan and spread evenly on top of the bottom layer.
4. Add a second layer of Kibbeh on top of the stuffing. Spread it evenly. Score the top layer with a sharp knife in a crisscrossing pattern.
5. Glaze the top with melted butter. Bake at 350 degrees for 1 hour.

Oven-Baked Salmon with Olive Oil and Salt

Not even sushi is as quick and easy as this oven-baked salmon recipe. You can prep the salmon in just a couple of minutes, and it only needs to cook for a short time. While the salmon is baking, you can throw together a quick salad—like perhaps a Spinach Salad—and heat up a couple of rounds of Za'atar Bread in the oven after the salmon comes out. Depending on the thickness of the salmon, you could have a complete meal on the table in under 30 minutes.

There are so many different ways you can bake salmon. You can add black pepper, dill, fennel, mint, citrus, leeks, and even mustards. And you are certainly free to engage your creativity according to your tastes. But today I am going to share this very simple recipe for oven-baked salmon that really draws out the natural flavors of the salmon. It's so simple! You just need extra-virgin olive oil and salt.

Please note that I do not include in the recipe a specific time for the fillet to cook. That's because the cook-time really depends on the thickness of the salmon you have. So how do you know when the salmon is done? A general rule of thumb is to bake salmon for 4 to 6 minutes per ½-inch thickness. Salmon is done as soon as it begins to flake, and you can easily test the doneness by inserting a fork into the fish and gently twisting. If it starts to flake, it's done. Two other signs of doneness to look for: the flesh will be opaque and the juices will turn a milky-white.

INGREDIENTS

1 to 2 pounds salmon fillet, with the skin on (we prefer a wild-caught salmon, like a sockeye, but farm-raised bakes well too)

Extra-virgin olive oil (a generous pour to coat the top of the salmon)

Coarse ground kosher salt

INSTRUCTIONS

1. Preheat oven to 450 degrees.
2. Rinse salmon in fresh cold water, then pat dry.
3. Place salmon in a glass or ceramic baking dish, skin side down.
4. Coat with extra-virgin olive oil, then generously sprinkle with kosher salt.
5. Bake until opaque and flaky.

Vegetarian Entrees

Smothered Okra and Tomatoes, see page 186

Falafel

This recipe comes from my friend Chef Nabil M. Aho, member of Chefs for Peace and Head Culinary Instructor at the culinary institute attached to The Pontifical Institute Notre Dame of Jerusalem Center, the hotel where we stayed in Jerusalem. I made a few minor modifications to the recipe to adapt it to a home kitchen.

So what exactly is Falafel? Falafel is a fried croquette made out of chickpeas, just like Hummus. They are brown, crunchy, and delicious on the outside, and soft, green, and delicious on the inside. The Falafel "dough" is usually seasoned with garlic, cumin, cayenne, cinnamon, cardamom, and sumac, in addition to salt and black pepper. The green color comes from a combination of finely chopped parsley and cilantro.

And I'm embarrassed to say that I refused to eat Falafel until about two years ago. I am still suffering from residual *pickiness*, a condition that wreaked havoc on my childhood, at least culinarily. Thankfully, my wife won't stand for that. So two years ago we were in a local Greek/Lebanese restaurant called Albasha, and my wife wanted to order Falafel as an appetizer. I must have made a face when she suggested Falafel, because the next thing I know, I'm being issued a challenge. The Falafel were brought to the table with a Tahini Sauce for dipping. I tasted and I swooned. "Why haven't I had these before?" I thought. They were so good I wanted to order more!

Since then, we routinely order the Falafel when we eat at that restaurant, but I had never made Falafel myself until that day in Jerusalem at the culinary institute attached to the Notre Dame Hotel. Chef Nabil is passionate about good food and about the culture that food conveys. And when Pope Francis journeyed to the Holy Land in May of 2014, guess who was one of the chefs privileged to cook for the Pope. That's right. Chef Nabil!

I should point out that, unlike Hummus, you do not cook the chickpeas for Falafel after soaking them overnight. Falafel can be served simply with Creamy Tahini Sauce and hot Pita as part of a Mezze, or you can use them to make a sandwich. See the next recipe for suggestions on making a Falafel sandwich.

INGREDIENTS

2 cups dried chickpeas

1 medium sweet yellow onion, finely chopped

1 bunch of parsley, finely chopped

½ bunch of cilantro, finely chopped

5 cloves of garlic "with jacket" (can also use roasted garlic)

1 to 2 tablespoons of flour

1 teaspoon cumin

1 ½ teaspoons kosher salt

½ teaspoon freshly cracked black pepper

½ teaspoon cayenne pepper

½ teaspoon cinnamon

¼ teaspoon ground cardamom

1 teaspoon sumac

1 teaspoon baking powder

Raw radish leaves (optional)

4 cups of vegetable oil for frying

INSTRUCTIONS

1. Place chickpeas in a large bowl and cover with cold water by about 3 inches. Let them soak overnight. The chickpeas will basically double in size overnight, so you will end up with about 4 cups of soaked chickpeas.

2. Drain and rinse the soaked chickpeas and put them in a food processor with the onions, garlic, parsley, and cilantro. Pulse

until fully mixed into a dough. You are looking for something like the consistency of paste. You want it to hold together, but you don't want it to be too smooth.

3. Add the spices along with the baking powder and flour. Pulse to integrate. Transfer to a large bowl, cover with plastic wrap, then place the bowl in the refrigerator and let it rest for one to two hours.

4. Heat the oil in a deep skillet over medium heat.

5. Shape the Falafel mixture into small "balls" that fit in the palm of your hand, about the size of a large walnut. But you can make them larger or smaller, according to your taste. Instead of rolling them by hand, you can use a Falafel scoop.

6. Fry in batches of 5 or 6 for 2 to 3 minutes per side. Total cook time should be about 5 minutes per batch. Remove from oil with a slotted spoon and drain on paper towels.

7. Serve Falafel hot. It can be served with Hummus (page 34) or with Tahini Sauce (page 44). Falafel also make a great sandwich. *See page 178 for Falafel sandwich ideas.*

NOTE: FIXING FALAFEL
If the Falafel will not hold together after letting it rest in the refrigerator, you can stir in additional flour to the mixture a tablespoon at a time. You shouldn't have to exceed 3 tablespoons.

Falafel-Stuffed Pita Sandwiches

Our Falafel lunch with Chef Nabil and the culinary students was fun, but it was more than that. Something about it resonated with me and reminded me of home. Maybe it was the fact that the kitchen was big enough to accommodate everybody. There were no chairs, so everyone was standing around talking, making Falafel, and eating. That is often the norm down in south Louisiana. It is not uncommon for family and friends to hang out in the kitchen talking and cooking together, and there is always something to snack on. Even wedding receptions down here are generally standup affairs.

The first day I arrived in The Holy Land, I ended up having breakfast with most of our group (some of them straggled in later than the rest of the group) and our guide Arlette Kara'a. Over the course of our 11-day pilgrimage, Arlette quickly and effectively touched my heart. She became a dear friend and a sister to me. On traditional pilgrimages, the protocol is for the guides to eat separately from the groups. This goes for all travel companies. Meals provide a necessary break—downtime—for both the groups and the guides. But I had a hard time reconciling this myself since our pilgrimage was specifically a Food Meets Faith pilgrimage focusing on growing in faith around the table—the table of the Eucharist and the family table at home. Besides, in my eyes, Arlette was part of the group. But the only time we were all able to eat together was at that lunch with Chef Nabil. There was so much joy in that kitchen. It was beautiful.

Besides Arlette, I met another special friend on that pilgrimage: our driver Adel. He is Muslim, and he is a good man. Adel spoke English very well, and he and I conversed a lot during the pilgrimage. He became my friend. Without realizing it, Adel showed me again how much food plays a part in our families and friendships. At this Falafel lunch, when everybody was together in the kitchen eating, Adel made an offer. As I went to grab a Pita to start making my sandwich, Adel stopped me, put his hand on my shoulder, and said, "No, my friend. Allow me. I will make you the best Falafel sandwich in the world." It was a simple gesture. Kind. And it perfectly accentuated the fact that we humans are drawn to relationship, to friendship, and a big part of friendship is sharing food.

I'm sure those thoughts weren't going through Adel's mind as he made my sandwich, but they were going through mine, and I was touched. He was right, by the way. It was the best Falafel sandwich in the world.

INGREDIENTS

Arabic Bread (Pita), cut in half to form two "pockets"

3 to 4 Falafel (per sandwich)

Any combination of the following traditional add-ons:

Hummus
Tahini Sauce
Labneh
Pickled turnips or other pickles
Chopped or shredded Romaine lettuce
Sliced tomatoes

Red or yellow onions
Srirachi or some other chili sauce
French fries

INSTRUCTIONS

1. Apply a layer of Hummus, Labneh or Tahini Sauce in the pocket of the Pita. Place 3 or 4 Falafel in the pocket, then add any of the other ingredients you like. Enjoy!

Mint, Egg, and Onion Omelet

Breakfast is the most important meal of the day. Adel and I discussed this fact over breakfast one morning in Nazareth. I was running a little late to breakfast. The group was already loading their bags in the bus because this was our last morning in Nazareth. Later in the afternoon we would travel to Jerusalem.

"Eating breakfast," Adel told me, "tells your body that it has work to do. I never miss breakfast. It's the most important meal of the day." I heartily agreed.

Omelets aren't only for breakfast though. There is many a night in my kitchen when I opt to serve breakfast for dinner. After coming in late from gymnastics practice and karate, scrambling eggs or throwing together a quick omelet can keep peace in the heart and food on the table. The key word here is *quick*.

Mint grows like a weed. If you're not careful it can overtake portions of your yard or garden. I joke about having a *black thumb*, because I really haven't had much success with gardening. Most things I plant die. But even me and my black thumb can grow mint.

Onions and eggs go together well, but you might be surprised to think of mint and eggs going together. But they do. Sometimes I'll even add Za'atar to my eggs, whether scrambled or cooked as an omelet.

One of my culinary heroes is Alton Brown. I used to love watching his show *Good Eats*. It was so creative and educational. I learned tons from Alton over the years. I remember watching an episode called The Eggs Files, an obvious takeoff of The X-Files. What I saw on that episode revolutionized the way that I cook and eat eggs.

Here are a few examples:

- I now heat my plates while the eggs are cooking so that I serve hot eggs on warm plates. That little extra step makes all the difference.
- Eggs over-easy are cooked low and slow, flipping only once. The second side only needs 45 to 60 seconds to cook.
- Scrambled eggs are cooked more quickly, and at a higher heat. I often use butter, bacon drippings, or coconut oil instead of olive oil when cooking any version of eggs in a skillet. The recipe below will make two omelets.

INGREDIENTS

6 eggs

2 tablespoons parsley, finely chopped

2 tablespoons flour

2 tablespoons mint leaves, finely chopped

4 green onions, chopped

4 tablespoons extra virgin olive oil

Kosher salt and freshly cracked black pepper, to taste

Crumbled Feta cheese, as garnish (optional)

INSTRUCTIONS

1. Crack the eggs into a mixing bowl. Add the parsley, mint, and green onions. Whisk together well.
2. In a skillet over medium heat, drizzle some of the olive oil.
3. Pour about half of the egg mixture into the skillet, season with a pinch of kosher salt and black pepper to taste, and fry for about 3 minutes. Using a spatula, flip the omelet over and fry the other side for about 3 minutes.
4. Remove to a plate and serve hot. Optionally, you can garnish with a bit of crumbled Feta cheese.

Shakshuka
(Spicy Tomato Sauce with Eggs)

This was the first dish that I tasted in the Holy Land. Because of that snowstorm on the East Coast our departure from the United States was delayed and caused our routes to change. We were supposed to have a direct flight from New York to Tel Aviv. That didn't happen. In fact, our group was split up. I traveled via Atlanta and Amsterdam to Tel Aviv. The rest of the group traveled to Houston, then Frankfurt, to Tel Aviv. As a result, we didn't get to our hotel in Natanya until the wee hours of the morning. Although I was exhausted, I did not go to sleep. Instead, I washed up, made a pot of coffee, read from the Bible, and spent some time in prayer.

Breakfast was served buffet-style, and everything looked so fresh and...Middle Eastern. This wasn't any American buffet, and I loved that it wasn't. Hummus, several different cheeses including Labneh, various types of Pita, fresh vegetables, and many other dishes lined the tables. It was a breakfast feast! I had never seen or heard of Shakshuka before that morning, but I was drawn to it because it reminded me of the Shrimp Creole we cook at home, except with eggs instead of shrimp. Simply put, Shakshuka is a spicy tomato sauce with chunks of onions, bell pepper, and garlic. It's heat comes from jalapeños or crushed red pepper flakes, or a combination of both. Once the sauce cooks down to a decent thickness, indentations are made on the surface with a cooking spoon, and eggs are cracked and dropped into the indentations and cooked to your desired doneness. The Italians have a similar dish they call Eggs in Purgatory. It's spicy. But I like the heat.

INGREDIENTS

3 tablespoons extra virgin olive oil

2 medium sweet yellow onions, chopped

3 cloves of garlic, minced

1 large red bell pepper, chopped

2 jalapeño peppers, seeded and chopped

4 cups ripe tomatoes, diced (or 1 28 oz. can of whole plum tomatoes, crushed by hand)

2 tablespoons tomato paste

1 tablespoon chili powder

1 tablespoon cumin

1 teaspoon paprika

½ to 1 teaspoon cayenne, or to taste

1/3 teaspoon turmeric

1 teaspoon sugar, or to taste

Kosher salt and freshly cracked black pepper, to taste

1 cup of chopped fresh spinach

6 eggs

6 ounces of Feta cheese, cut into small 1/2-inch cubes

Fresh chopped parsley or cilantro, as garnish

INSTRUCTIONS

1. Heat the oil in a large skillet over medium-high heat. Add the onions and peppers and sauté until softened, about 8 minutes.

2. Add the garlic, tomato paste, chili powder, cumin, paprika, cayenne, turmeric, salt, and black pepper. Stir well to incorporate. Continue to sauté, stirring frequently, until garlic is softened and

tomato paste is fully incorporated, about 2 minutes.

3. Add tomatoes and their juice, stirring to incorporate. Stir in the sugar and reduce heat to medium and simmer, stirring occasionally, until the sauce is thickened slightly, about 20 minutes. You don't want the sauce to be too thick, but you don't want it to be too watery either. The goal is for the sauce to be thick enough to form individual "bowls" for the eggs to cook in. Taste and adjust seasoning as necessary.

4. Stir in the fresh chopped spinach.

5. Turn the heat down to low, and press the cubes of Feta—evenly—into the tomato sauce. Using the back of a spoon, make 6 indentations in the sauce, and crack an egg into each indentation.

6. Turn the heat back up to a gentle simmer for about 10 minutes. Gently "baste" the eggs occasionally with a spatula, being careful not to break the yolks. Cover and cook to your liking, which shouldn't take longer than 3 to 5 minutes.

7. Serve on plates, garnish with freshly chopped parsley or cilantro. Arabic Bread, or crusty French Bread, goes really well with this dish.

Photo Courtesy Diana von Glahn

Cauliflower with Tomatoes

I was amazed at the abundance of tomatoes in the Holy Land. They came in all shapes and sizes: grape, cherry, plum, and beefsteak. They were all fresh and bursting with flavor.

This is a great summer recipe when tomatoes are in season, but you can make it any time of the year by using canned tomatoes.

Believe it or not, cauliflower wasn't introduced to the United States until the early 1900s. It's indigenous to the Middle East and Asia, but the vast majority of cauliflower grown in the United States is grown in California. Because of the California climate, farmers are able to grown cauliflower almost year-round. It's one of those cruciferous vegetables I spent most of my life turning my nose up at, and it's related to broccoli, cabbage, kale, turnips, rutabagas, and Brussels sprouts.

It took me a while to come around, but I'm part of the Cauliflower Club now. Oh, did I mention it is really, really good for you too?

INGREDIENTS

1 large head of cauliflower, cut into florets

3 large ripe tomatoes, diced (can substitute 1 28 oz. can of petite diced tomatoes)

1 medium sweet yellow onion, chopped

1 teaspoon allspice

1 teaspoon cinnamon

1 teaspoon sugar

Kosher salt, to taste

4 tablespoons butter

INSTRUCTIONS

1. In a skillet over medium-high heat, sauté the cauliflower in butter until it begins to lightly brown. Remove and set aside.
2. In the same skillet, sauté the onion in butter until it becomes translucent, about 8 to 10 minutes.
3. Add the tomatoes to the skillet, stirring to incorporate. Bring to a simmer and allow to simmer until slightly reduced, about 15 minutes.
4. Add the cauliflower to the skillet and cook on low to medium-low for about 30 minutes, until the cauliflower has softened.
5. Adjust seasonings to taste.

Smothered Okra and Tomatoes

When I was a kid, I hated okra. I would even pick it out of my gumbo and set it on a plate or a paper napkin. But my mother loved okra, and my grandfather grew it in his garden. So okra was always on our summer menus, much to my dismay.

I am happy to say things have changed. I now eat okra in my gumbo. As a matter of fact, one of my favorite gumbos is Shrimp & Okra Gumbo. It's easy to make, and it's delicious in the summer when both shrimp and okra are in season.

I can't say that I would normally opt for okra on any given day. Until now, that is.

A couple of summers ago, my wife made Smothered Okra & Tomatoes based on Emeril Lagasse's recipe in his book *Louisiana Real & Rustic*. I remember tasting it. It was pretty good. She also fried okra last summer, just for fun. I ate that too. And I liked it. I used okra several times in gumbo over the course of the fall and winter. But that was frozen okra we bought at the supermarket. I really only had fresh okra for the first time a couple of summers ago...just to appease my wife.

My wife asked me to pick up fresh okra from the farmers market. "OK..." was my hesitant response. I was wondering if I was going to be expected to eat it again. Funny how quickly we can forget some things. "You loved it last summer when I smothered it with tomatoes." she said. "That's right!" I said. "How could I forget that?"

So, off to the market I went, and fresh okra did I purchase. Now this is one of my favorite summer recipes, Okra with Tomatoes & Onions. I was also pleasantly surprised to see okra (and even okra and tomatoes together) served in the Holy Land. It is truly the land of milk and honey...and okra.

INGREDIENTS

1 ½ pounds okra, rinsed, dried, tops cut off, sliced into 1/2-inch rounds

3 large ripe tomatoes, diced (can substitute 1 28 oz. can of petite diced tomatoes)

2 medium yellow onions, chopped

2 cloves of garlic, minced

1 teaspoon kosher salt, or to taste

Freshly cracked black pepper to taste

¼ of cayenne, or to taste

4 tablespoons of butter

Rice (cooked according to package directions)

INSTRUCTIONS

1. In a skillet over medium-high heat, sauté the onions in butter until translucent, about 8 to 10 minutes. Add the garlic and sauté for an additional minute or two, stirring constantly.
2. Add the tomatoes, salt, pepper, and cayenne. Bring to boil, reduce heat and simmer, covered, for about 15 to 20 minutes.
3. In the meantime, in a separate skillet, pan fry the okra in butter until lightly browned. You will probably need to do this in batches.
4. Add the okra to the tomatoes and simmer until the okra is tender, about 15 minutes.
5. Serve over hot rice.

Desserts

Sesame Tahini Paste Cookies, see page 196

Baklava

Baklava is a pastry made with layers of phyllo dough, filled with chopped nuts and a sweet syrup. It is also probably the most well-known Middle Eastern dessert in the United States. It's a standard on the menus in Greek and Lebanese restaurants, but Baklava can be claimed as a national dessert by many countries the Mediterranean area, and each country or region has a different way of making it. For example, in The Holy Land orange and lemon rind used in the syrup, whereas in Lebanon orange water or rose water are used instead. In Greece, Baklava is made with 33 layers of phyllo dough in honor of the 33 years of Jesus' life.

Phyllo dough is the most unusual element of the dessert, and working with phyllo can be quite a challenge. When my wife's family makes Baklava there are 5 or 6 women in the kitchen assembling the Baklava, carefully handling sheets of paper-thin phyllo, trying to avoid tearing it. Once each layer was in place, melted butter was applied with a brush to prevent the dough from drying out. It's what we call a "labor of love."

The recipe below comes from the dessert makers at the New Orleans Greek Festival, which is presented by the Holy Trinity Greek Orthodox Cathedral in New Orleans every Memorial Day weekend. I am sharing share the recipe here with their permission. In 2014 the Holy Trinity Greek Orthodox Cathedral is celebrating its 150th year in New Orleans! Founded in 1864, this community is the first Greek Orthodox Church in the Americas.

In addition to that celebration, something else occurred during this year's Greek Festival that made it extra-special for me. That very same weekend Pope Francis met with Patriarch Bartholomew of Constantinople in Jerusalem! That meeting commemorated the meeting between the Patriarch of Constantinople Athenagoras and Pope Paul VI in 1964 in Jerusalem...50 years ago! We are so close to our Orthodox brothers and sisters, and we long for the day when we will be one again.

Recipe courtesy of Greek Festival New Orleans and Holy Trinity Cathedral.

Baklava Syrup (Make this First)

INGREDIENTS

6 cups sugar

4 cups water

Juice of ½ lemon

3 cinnamon sticks

5 whole cloves

2 tablespoons honey

INSTRUCTIONS

(Makes about 32 pieces of baklava)

1. Combine sugar, water, lemon, cinnamon, and cloves in a large saucepan and bring mixture to a boil.
2. Reduce heat and simmer over medium heat, uncovered, for 25 to 30 minutes.
3. Turn off heat and stir in honey until dissolved. Let syrup cool at room temperature and chill.

Baklava

INGREDIENTS

2 pounds of unsalted butter

2 pounds of frozen phyllo, thawed in the box

7 cups coarsely chopped walnuts

¼ cup sugar

2 heaping tablespoons ground cinnamon

INSTRUCTIONS

1. Preheat oven to 300 degrees
2. Remove thawed phyllo from boxes and arrange on a work surface and cover with a damp kitchen towel.

3. Melt butter in a medium saucepan and skim away and discard the foam from the top. Pour off the melted butter into another saucepan, leaving behind and discarding the water from the butter.

4. Butter an 18 x 13-inch baking sheet. Arrange one layer of phyllo in pan and butter phyllo. Make 11 more layers in the same manner, being sure to butter the phyllo well.

5. In a bowl combine walnuts, sugar, and cinnamon. Sprinkle a cup of the nut mixture over the phyllo and top with three layers of phyllo, buttering in between each layer of phyllo. Continue to make more layers in the same manner until all the nuts are used. Arrange 14 sheets of phyllo over the last of the nuts, being sure to butter between each layer of phyllo

well. With a sharp knife cut Baklava into diamonds or triangles about 2 inches in diameter.

6. Bake Baklava in the center of the oven for 2 hours, or until golden brown. If the Baklava browns too quickly reduce oven to 275 degrees. Remove from oven and immediately pour chilled syrup over hot Baklava.

NOTE:

The trick to a moist—but not soggy—Baklava is to pour cold syrup onto hot Baklava.

Knafeh

Knafeh is an amazing dessert. It's a sweet cheese pastry soaked in syrup which I first tasted on the bus in Nazareth. It was the first real day in the Holy Land. That morning we celebrated Mass in the shrine of Our Lady of Mount Carmel on, well, Mount Carmel. Then we made our way to Cana of Galilee where we had ceremony for the renewal of wedding vows, followed by a visit to the shop of a local Christian family, where we sample some of the wines made right there in Cana. Then we made the curvy uphill and downhill drive from Cana to Nazareth, where we stopped to pray at the stunning Church of the Annunciation. This church commemorates the spot where the angel Gabriel appeared to the Virgin Mary. There is an altar and a stone that marks the very spot where God became flesh. The plaque there reads, "And the Word was made flesh here." That *here* had a powerful affect on me and many others in the group. We were standing next to the spot where the world was completely changed forever.

During the day, Adel our driver had been telling me about his favorite dessert, Knafeh. I was intrigued and told him that I would love to try it. Well, as it turns out, when we were driving to the hotel in the late afternoon traffic, Adel spotted some friends of his in a car a few links ahead. He pulled out his cell phone and made a quick call in Arabic. Then he turned to me and said, "My friend, today you will try Knafeh and you will love it." I said, "Great! When?" He smiled and said, "Right now." Just then I saw a young man running toward the bus, and he was carrying a bag. He ran up to the Adel's window and handed him the bag, then waved to me. Adel handed me the bag, and inside was Knafeh. It was still warm, and it was so good. It reminded me of an éclair, it was like a cylinder, and it was topped with what looked like shredded phyllo dough. I later learned that it could have been a type of long, thin noodle threads. Did I mention that it was amazing? The paper bag, and the fact that it had been personally delivered to me on the street, left me with the impression of Knafeh as street food, although that might not necessarily be the case. At The Green Valley, Knafeh is served as dessert in a restaurant, and it looked very different. It was made right in front of us and heated on a large metal tray over a propane flame. Different shape and size, but it still tasted like the first Knafeh I had eaten.

The recipe below is more like the Knafeh from The Green Valley. It's not complicated to make, but you will need to get your hands on shredded phyllo dough. It's called Kadaif.

INGREDIENTS

For the Syrup
1 ½ cups sugar

1 tablespoon lemon juice

1 teaspoon rose water

1 cup of water

For the Knafeh
1 cup whole milk

1 cup heavy whipping cream

2 teaspoons rose water

1 pound ricotta cheese

½ pound Kadaif noodles (shredded phyllo dough)

1 tablespoon sugar

1 tablespoons cornstarch

¾ cup unsalted butter

1/3 cup pistachios, chopped

INSTRUCTIONS

Make the Syrup

1. Combine sugar, water, lemon juice, and rose water in a saucepan over medium heat.
2. Bring to a boil, stirring constantly.
3. Reduce heat and simmer on low for 15 to 20 minutes. You want to reduce the syrup until it is thick enough to coat a spoon.
4. Remove from heat, let cool, then refrigerate until ready to use.

Make the Knafeh

1. Preheat oven to 350 degrees.
2. In a saucepan over medium heat, combine the milk, the cream, the sugar, and the cornstarch. Stir until the sugar and cornstarch are dissolved.
3. Once the mixture begins to boil, add the rose water and stir. Reduce heat to low and simmer for 5 to 10 minutes, or until it thickens.
4. Remove from heat and let cool. Once cool, stir in the ricotta cheese until fully incorporated.
5. Shred the noodles in a bowl by hand, or use a food processor to pulse them just enough to break them up and separate them.
6. Melt butter over low heat, then pour over the shredded phyllo dough. Mix together thoroughly by hand.
7. Line the bottom of a 9 x 13-inch baking dish with butter and phyllo dough mixture, firmly flattening it to even it out to the edges of the dish.
8. Evenly spread the ricotta cheese mixture over the shredded phyllo dough and butter mixture, then top with the remaining phyllo dough mixture. Press down gently on the topping.
9. Place the baking dish in the oven, uncovered, and bake for 1 hour, or until the top is golden.
10. Remove the Knafeh from the oven and immediately pour the cold syrup on the hot Knafeh. Sprinkle chopped pistachios on top, cut, and serve immediately.

Lebanese Butter Cookies—Ghraybi (or Ghraybeh)

Delicate. That's how I would describe these cookies. Delicate with a soft, understated sweetness. These cookies certainly make an impression for any occasion, though for us they are an annual Christmas tradition. There's nothing like tradition to bind a family together, and our family is no exception. We have lots of traditions that bind us together. Whether it's the annual birthday crawfish boils for my girls, going to our favorite Mardi Gras parades every year, or attending the Greek Festival in New Orleans every May, these are things we do together every year, and we always look forward to them. Advent and Christmas are the same way. We have our in-home traditions of the Advent wreath and our favorite novenas and prayers, but we also have some "foodie" traditions, like these Lebanese Butter Cookies. As a matter of fact, these cookies are a sign to us that Christmas is near.

My wife is Lebanese, and every year at Christmas family gatherings, her Aunt Rita used to make her special version of these cookies…in the shape of a camel. Aunt Rita passed away a few years ago, so the following Christmas Char (my wife) wanted to carry on the tradition. Although these cookies aren't exactly like Aunt Rita's, the taste is so similar and they say "Christmas" to us. We miss Aunt Rita, and we think that she would be happy to see that these butter cookies—and memories of her—are still very much a part of our family Christmases.

INGREDIENTS
- 1 cup clarified butter, chilled in refrigerator until congealed
- 1 cup sugar
- ½ cup all-purpose flour (to start)
- 1 cup blanched almonds, optional

INSTRUCTIONS
1. Preheat oven to 300 degrees.
2. Clarify the butter in a heavy-bottomed saucepan over very low heat until melted. Allow the butter to simmer gently. Foam will rise to the surface. When it looks like no more foam is being produced, remove the saucepan from heat and skim and discard the foam (or save it to use in other recipes).
3. Slowly pour the butter into a heat-proof container, careful to leave behind the milk solids in the bottom of the saucepan. Alternatively, you can strain the butter through a few layers of cheesecloth.
4. Place butter in the refrigerator until congealed, then remove from the fridge and allow to come to room temperature.
5. In a stand mixer (or with a handheld mixer) cream the butter (see details below) until fluffy, about 5 minutes. Add the sugar and continue creaming an additional 5 minutes. Add ½ cup flour and continue to mix until smooth. If the dough is too sticky, add a little more flour a bit at a time. You shouldn't need to add any more than an additional ½ cup.
6. Pinch off a small piece dough to fit in the palm of your hand. Shape it into a ½ inch round, like a little ball, and place it on an ungreased cookie sheet or baking stone. Repeat this process with the remaining dough. If you so desire, you can gently press down the center of each cookie with your thumb and place a blanched almond in the indention.
7. Bake in the oven at 300 degrees for 13 to 15 minutes. The cookies will be very pale in color. Gently transfer them to a cooling rack and allow them to cool for 6 hours before serving. These cookies are very flaky. They will easily fall apart if you try to move them when they are warm.

NOTE: How to Properly Cream Butter

To cream butter well, the butter has to first be softened at room temperature. You will know that the butter is soft enough when it offers little resistance to a knife. Just don't over-soften the butter. Melted, oily butter does not cream well.

Using a hand mixer, beat the butter on low speed briefly, making it creamy. Add in the sugar and continue beating on low to combine. Once the sugar and butter are combined, increase the speed to medium and continue beating. Continuing to beat the butter results in increased volume. The butter will become creamy and start to pale. Properly creamed butter has an off-white color.

Sesame Tahini Paste Cookies

My daughters love to bake cookies from scratch. Usually, they bake chocolate chip cookies or sugar cookies. We tried these after I got back from the Holy Land because they were so similar to some of the cookies that we enjoy every year at the Greek Festival in New Orleans. I like the addition of tahini in this recipe. It gives the cookies an unexpected, yet pleasant, quality, almost like peanut butter cookies, but lighter and crispier.

INGREDIENTS

1¼ cups all-purpose flour

½ teaspoon baking powder

¼ teaspoon kosher salt

1 stick unsalted butter, softened at room temperature

½ cup granulated sugar

½ cup tahini, well blended

1 teaspoon pure vanilla extract

⅓ cup sesame seeds

INSTRUCTIONS

1. Preheat oven to 350 degrees.
2. In a mixing bowl, combine the flour, baking powder, and salt, and mix together well.
3. In the work bowl of a stand mixer, beat together the butter and sugar until pale and fluffy, about 3 minutes. Then add the tahini and the vanilla extract. Beat to incorporate. Reduce speed of the mixer and begin to add the flour mixture in batches, continuing to mix until it forms a crumbly dough.
4. Transfer the dough to a work surface covered with plastic wrap. Press the dough into a disk, wrap it in the plastic and refrigerate it for about an hour, or until it becomes firm.
5. Line 2 large baking sheets with parchment paper. It's best to alternate baking sheets since you will not be able to fit all the cookies on one sheet.
6. Place the sesame seeds in a bowl.
7. Remove dough from refrigerator and pull pieces from the dough and roll them out into 1-inch balls. Then roll each ball in the sesame seeds and place on baking sheet, arranging the cookies about 2 inches apart.
8. Bake at 350 degrees for 12 to 15 minutes, until the cookies are puffed up and start to crack. Remove from oven and allow to cool on baking sheet for about 10 minutes before transferring to a cooling rack.

Harisa (Semolina Cake)

This is such a fun cake to make. It's very different from any cake I have made before and I was curious to see how it worked. It is made with semolina flour or farina, which is sold as Cream of Wheat in the United States. This cake was a hit with the whole family.

I am always intrigued by desserts that use ingredients that you wouldn't expect. For instance, the semolina flour (or Cream of Wheat) in this recipe and the tahini in the Sesame Tahini Paste Cookies. A little love and a little sugar can work magic when combing untraditional dessert ingredients. I like that.

Rose water is something that you can find in Middle Eastern markets and online. It really does come from rose petals and it smells just like roses. It is used in Middle Eastern recipes, particularly some of the desserts.

Pouring either hot syrup over cold cake, or cold syrup over hot cake, works like magic. The effects are impressive.

INGREDIENTS

For the Syrup:
- 1 ½ cups water
- 1 ⅓ cups granulated sugar
- 2 tablespoons rose water
- 2 teaspoon lemon juice
- 2 tablespoons orange blossom water

For the Cake:
- 14 oz. of semolina flour (can also use farina, like Cream of Wheat)
- 1 cup granulated sugar
- 1 cup full-fat Greek yogurt
- 2 sticks unsalted butter, melted and cooled
- 2 tablespoons baking powder
- 1 tablespoon tahini paste
- 1 tablespoon vanilla extract
- ½ cup pistachios, chopped

INSTRUCTIONS

For the Syrup:
1. In a medium saucepan over medium-high heat, combine the water, the sugar, the rose water, and orange blossom water, and the lemon juice.
2. Bring to boil, then lower the heat slightly, and allow to cook for about 20 to 25 minutes.

For the Cake:
1. Preheat the oven to 350 degrees, and place a rack in the upper 1/3 of the oven.
2. In a large mixing bowl, mix together the semolina flour (or farina), baking powder, granulated sugar, yogurt, melted butter, the vanilla extract, and 3 tablespoons of the syrup. Mix together well and set aside for at least 30 minutes.
3. Grease a baking dish with tahini paste (or use butter). Transfer the semolina mixture to the baking dish and spread evenly. Score the top to make 20 pieces.
4. Bake at 350 degrees for about 20 minutes, then turn the broiler on for 1 to 2 minutes to make the top golden brown.
5. Remove cake from oven and allow to cool.
6. When the cake is cooled, pour hot syrup over the cake. Please note that you will probably not use all of the syrup. You can cover the extra and store in the refrigerator for up to 4 months.
7. Serve the cake on plates and garnish with crushed pistachios.

Turkish Coffee

Coffee. It's one of my favorite things in the world. I like it strong and dark, and I'm typically not disappointed down here in south Louisiana. Around here dark coffee is the norm.

Espresso is a popular Italian coffee here in the United States, and Turkish coffee is similar to Espresso in many ways. Both are very fine grinds of dark coffee beans, but Turkish coffee is finer. It's ground almost to a powder. When making Espresso, hot water is filtered through the grinds, but to make Turkish Coffee the grinds are added to boiling water. The grinds end up in the cups too—typically small demitasse cups—which is why you need to let it sit for a minute before drinking to give the grinds the opportunity to settle.

I never had to worry about finding coffee when I was in the Holy Land. In addition to an abundance of coffee shops in every city, there were also men in the larger cities selling coffee on the sides of the road, serving it from large brass ibriks with smoke wafting from top compartment where the charcoal heated the whole container to keep the coffee warm. I enjoyed every cup.

Cardamom is usually added to Turkish Coffee. That aromatic spice adds an exotic flavor to the coffee. Two of my first purchases after returning from the Holy Land were a small ibrik to make Turkish Coffee on my stove and a jar of fresh cardamom pods. I find that a Turkish Coffee is the perfect beverage to enjoy in the mid-afternoon hours. Of course, it can be served at any time of the day. Making Turkish Coffee is a unique and different process. It may take some practice before you get used to it, but it will be time well spent.

INGREDIENTS
1 cup of water

1 tablespoon Turkish-ground coffee (an extra finely ground coffee)

1 cardamom pod

Sugar (optional)

NOTE:
You don't want to stir Turkish coffee after it is poured into the cup, so—if desired—it is best to add sugar in the beginning when bringing the water to a boil.

INSTRUCTIONS
1. Bring water to a boil in a small saucepan (or an ibrik, if you have one).
2. Remove the saucepan from heat and add the coffee and cardamom pod.
3. Return to heat and allow to come to a boil, but be careful not to let it boil over. Remove from heat again when the coffee foams.
4. Return to the heat until it foams, and remove again.
5. Pour into cups (demitasse cups) and allow to settle for a minute or two before drinking. Remember, there will be coffee grinds in the bottom of the cups.

Spiced Plum Cake

I live in Covington, which is on the "Northshore" of New Orleans. On the Northshore there is only one food truck, *LOLA Deux*, which is an extension of the LOLA Restaurant in Covington, and I have been frequenting LOLA for years.

LOLA is unique in many ways. It's located within the old train depot building right on the old railroad tracks in the middle of town. Amazingly enough, their kitchen is actually housed within a real train caboose!

My friends Chefs Keith and Nealy Frentz own and operate LOLA. They are both chefs and they are married...to each other. Nealy and Keith Frentz both graduated from the prestigious Johnson & Wales University with degrees in culinary arts. They then both worked at the iconic Brennan's restaurant in New Orleans. Hurricane Katrina was instrumental in the birth of LOLA because it forced Keith and Nealy to relocate to the Northshore. Talk about making something good out of something bad! It was only because of Hurricane Katrina that Keith and Nealy were able to make their dream a reality. They opened the doors of LOLA in Covington in January of 2006.

In May of 2012, Keith and Nealy Frentz were crowned as the King and Queen of Louisiana Seafood by the Louisiana Seafood Promotion & Marketing Board. That was the first time the crown from the Louisiana Seafood Cookoff went to a married couple. Prior to 2012, there was only a king OR a queen. Keith and Nealy changed that. They are such trendsetters.

Chef Nealy is known for her baking. She competed on Food Network's Chopped a few years ago, and she almost won. She was chopped in the last round—the dessert round of all things!—because she cut her finger and was disqualified. But she's still a winner in my book.

Since she is so good with desserts, I asked her for a recipe for this book. She sent me her Grammy Bertie's Spiced Plum Cake. If you want to make it Middle Eastern, you could always use dates instead of dried plums.

INGREDIENTS

3 eggs

1 cup vegetable oil

1 ½ cup sugar

1 teaspoon each cinnamon, nutmeg, allspice

1 teaspoon baking soda

1 cup buttermilk

2¼ cup flour

1 cup pitted prunes cooked (boil prunes in water until fork)

1 teaspoon vanilla extract

1 cup chopped walnuts

INSTRUCTIONS

1. Mix sugar and oil, and add eggs one at a time.
2. Put all dry ingredients into a bowl.
3. Alternate pouring the dry with the buttermilk into the egg/sugar mixture.
4. Add vanilla, nuts and cooked prunes.
5. Preheat oven to 300 degrees.
6. Grease down a glass pyrex dish and pour in your batter.
7. Bake for 30-45 minutes or until a knife comes out clean.

Ingredients for the Icing

1 cup sugar

½ buttermilk

1 tablespoons corn syrup

¼ cup butter

1 teaspoon vanilla

½ teaspoon baking soda

INSTRUCTIONS
1. Mix all ingredients together, stir well.
2. Boil mix until soft ball forms.
3. Pour over hot cake. (This is more of a glaze then an icing.)

NOTE:
Chef Nealy likes to prick the cake with a toothpick all over before pouring the glaze over.

Acknowledgements

There are so many people to thank and acknowledge for making this book a reality. It certainly wasn't a one-man show. Of course, this is the part where I get nervous. I'm bound to forget somebody. If I forget to thank you here, just stop by and I'll make you something good to eat, and I'll thank you in person.

First and foremost, I must thank the Lord: Father, Son, and Spirit Blest. Thanks to my wife for her patience, love, encouragement, and for the much needed kicks in the rear to help keep me on track. Thanks to my awesome kids: Christopher, Annabelle, and Grace. They are my biggest cheerleaders and my best recipe testers, and just by waking up the morning they show me what an amazing God we have.

I have learned so much about food, cooking, faith, and family from my parents and sister: Danny and Sandy Young, and Tracy Young Boykin. And from my in-laws: Dr. Charles and Toni Nolan, and Norman and Elizabeth Nolan.

To Edita Krunic and Susan Prendergast of Select International Tours, and Saliba Danho, Sam Danho, and Shibly Kando of Voice of Faith Tours, Diana von Glahn, Arlette Kara'a and Adel our bus driver: Thank you so much for opening my eyes to the beauty and grace of the Holy Land and the Living Stones that make it so special.

To Chefs for Peace for the work they are doing in the Middle East to bring about peace through food. They are an example we all need to follow. And to Chef Nabil M. Aho, Chef Kevork Alemian, Chef Moshe Basson, Chef Joseph Hanna, and Chef Ahmed Okla for passing on recipes to me.

To those who accompanied me on the very first Food Meets Faith pilgrimage: Father Michael Werkhoven, Bill and Julie Duncan, Juan and Brenda Kindelan, Gary and Nancy Shellenberger, Frank and Ann Lamanna, Marta Tetzeli, Audrey Tetzeli, Jim Cortese, and Ted Cortese.

To so many folks who have encouraged me in this endeavor as The Catholic Foodie™ over the years: Mike Lindner, Lisa Hendey, Captain Jeff Nielsen, Dane Falkner, Father Roderick Vonhogen and SQPN, Danielle Bean, Patrick Moore and so many others.

To some of my culinary mentors: Marcelle Bienvenu, Justin Wilson, John Besh, Emeril Lagasse, and Alton Brown.

To my co-hosts on the Around the Table Food Show: Monsignor Christopher Nalty and David Dawson. You inspire me grow culinarily and as a radio host. Thank you!

And, finally, to the good folks at Liguori Publications whose expertise has made this simple book into a work of art. Thank you Theresa, Mark, Mary, Suann, and so many others who had a hand in stirring the pot. My sincerest thanks!

A sneak peek from Sarah Vabulas'

(a.k.a. The Catholic Drinkie's)

upcoming book*

Nickname: Saint John's LeMint
Style: Pale Ale - Lemon & Mint added
Volume: 1 gallon

ALL GRAIN INGREDIENTS
 1.8 pounds 2-row Pale Malt

 0.5 pounds Caramel 10

Hops
 0.25 oz. Citra (10 min)

 0.25 oz. Citra (0 min)

Additives
 ⅛ oz. dried lemon peel (10 min)

 ¼ oz. spearmint (10 min)

 1 tsp. Yeast Nutrient (10 min)

Yeast
 Safale S-05

Other
 Sliced lemons for serving

ALL-GRAIN INSTRUCTIONS
1. Heat 3 quarts of water to 154 degrees. Add grains and steep for 60 minutes. Maintain temperature around 153-155 degrees by checking temperature every 10 minutes and turning on stovetop to medium when temperature falls below range.
2. Mash out grain for 10 minutes at 170 degrees. Meanwhile, heat 3 quarts of water in another pot to 170 degrees for sparging.

Sparge
 Slowly pour the 3 quarts of 170 degrees water over the grain bag in strainer and let drip into pot, combining with wort. Repeat rinse 2 times to extract all sugars and remove all grain from the wort.

Boil
 Bring wort to a boil. Set a 60-minute timer, adding hops according to schedule (above). At 10 minutes to end of boil, add yeast nutrient, lemon peel, and mint.

 At end of boil, cool to about 70 degrees and pour into glass jug. Top off with clean water to 1-gallon mark (if necessary). Pitch yeast and shake jug for 2 minutes to aerate. Attach blow-off hose and let ferment for 2 weeks.

Bottling
 After 2 weeks, bottle with priming sugar. Wait 10-14 days and enjoy with a slice of lemon.

WWW.CATHOLICDRINKIE.COM

Catholic DRINKIE
EST. 2010

WHERE FAITH MEETS BREW

Sarah Vabulas is an active Catholic voice in the often godless culture of beer. She uses her faith and her passion for home brew to reach out to people who may not otherwise hear about God and the Church.

The Catholic Drinkie's Guide to Home-Brewed Evangelism will be available in Summer 2015 at fine bookstores everywhere.
Learn more and pre-order at Liguori.org or by calling 800-325-9521.
ISBN: **9780764825798**